AN EXPOSITION ON EFFICACY OF HOMOEOPATHY IN SARCOIDOSIS WITH MIASMATIC CONCEPTS

DR. RAJNEESH KUMAR SHARMA

With gratitude and reverence,

To our parents - the architects of our existence!

To our family - the pillars of support that upheld us!

To our colleagues and friends - the steadfast allies who bolstered us!

And

To Homoeopathy - the nurturing embrace that enveloped us!

And

Unified, we merge into its essence!

Contents

Preface

"Sarcoidosis" denotes a perplexing granulomatous disorder of yet undetermined origin, posing a threat to life. This condition transcends geographical and demographic boundaries, affecting individuals of all races, sexes, and ages worldwide. Its unpredictable manifestation spans multiple organ systems, traversing conventional medical specialties and presenting challenges to practitioners across disciplines. While not common, sarcoidosis often precipitates significant organ degeneration in afflicted individuals. Like any other disease, sarcoidosis impacts the entire person irrespective of its cause, altering the patient's physiological and psychological landscape. Each patient exhibits a unique disease profile, characterized by specific mental and physical manifestations reflective of their individuality. This distinctiveness underscores the holistic nature of the ailment, with symptomatology influenced by underlying miasms driving the disease process.Given the elusive etiology of sarcoidosis, treatment poses considerable challenges. Relying solely on symptomatology for a cure is often insufficient, necessitating a deeper understanding of the fundamental disease mechanisms through the lens of homeopathy, particularly miasms. This comprehensive approach enables targeted eradication of the condition.Within this book, we delve into various facets of sarcoidosis, offering a historical review, an overview from a homeopathic perspective, definitions, incidence and prevalence rates, clinical staging, diagnosis methodologies, pathological differential diagnoses, and treatment modalities. The latter half of the book delves into the correlation between sarcoidosis and homeopathy, elucidating miasmatic analyses of associated signs and symptoms. Finally, comprehensive therapeutics and repertory tools for sarcoidosis are provided, facilitating its holistic homeopathic management.

(Dr. Rajneesh Kumar Sharma) 01-04-2024

Acknowledgements

I am profoundly grateful to Padm Shree Dr. (Prof. Emeritus) V. K. Gupta, Dr. (Prof. Emeritus) V. K. Khanna, and Dr. (Prof.) V. C. Acharya for their exceptional intellect, scientific perspective, unwavering guidance, continuous encouragement, and keen interest, which have consistently propelled me to strive diligently throughout my research endeavors. Without their mentorship, the progress in my studies of Homoeopathic Research would have been unattainable. I am deeply indebted to them for generously devoting their precious time to offer guidance amidst their incredibly busy schedules.

I extend my heartfelt appreciation to my friends and colleagues whose invaluable counsel has been a source of strength during this journey.

Lastly, I express my gratitude to my family, whose silent sacrifices and unwavering support have enabled me to pursue this undertaking. I also extend my thanks to the hospital personnel and acquaintances who have assisted me along the way.

(Dr. Rajneesh Kumar Sharma)

CHAPTER ONE

An Exposition on Efficacy of Homoeopathy in Sarcoidosis with Miasmatic Concepts

Sarcoidosis is a complex multisystem disease characterized by the formation of noncaseating granulomas, affecting various organs in the body. Its cause remains unknown, but it likely involves an inflammatory response to various agents in genetically susceptible individuals. The disease can lead to significant mental stress and organ failure. The illness can vary in severity, with episodic recurrences and remissions. Treatment is challenging due to the unknown etiology, requiring an understanding of the disease's basic phenomena, such as miasms, for proper eradication, especially in terms of Homoeopathy.

Though not common, it is often a disorder causing a deal of mental stress and worry to the patient, often leading to permanent failure or disabilities of the organs ultimately leading to the end of vital functions. 'Sarcoidosis', like another disease, affects the person as a whole irrespective of the cause. The whole economy of the patient is altered producing the signs of Sarcoidosis as well as a characteristic picture of the sick individual including mental and physicals specific to his personality.

This disease picture specific to that particular patient is always different from that of another one. This difference is due to his particular identity proving him to be an 'Individual'. The totality of symptoms depends upon the Miasms under-running the disease process in that individual. Sarcoidosis affects individuals uniquely, with symptoms depending on underlying miasms. Psora, the fundamental miasm, plays a significant role in altering physiology, while the combination of miasms like Syphilis and Sycosis contributes to tissue destruction and granuloma formation. The Psora being the fundamental miasm plays a maximum role in altering the physiology rendering the entire imbalance. While in combination with other miasms, it produces the worst stage of the sickness. The syphilis produces destruction of tissues. To combat it, Sycosis and Psora play their vital part. This combination in turn increases the destruction as well as new tissue formation too, producing granulomas and fibromas publishing the complete portrait of Sarcoidosis.

The illness can be self-limited or chronic, with episodic recrudescence and remissions. The course and prognosis may correlate with the mode of onset and the extent of the disease. This exposition examines the current understanding of sarcoidosis, including the epidemiology, etiology, immunopathogenesis, pathology, clinical manifestations, diagnosis, management, and prognosis, especially in terms of Homoeopathy.

Since the etiology of Sarcoidosis is not known, it becomes very difficult to treat it. Only based on symptomatology, the final cure is not always possible. Therefore it becomes necessary to understand its basic disease phenomenon in terms of Homoeopathy i.e. miasms and only then its proper eradication can be done.

CHAPTER TWO

SARCOIDOSIS – THE HISTORICAL REVIEW

The word "sarcoidosis" originates from the Greek word "sarkodes," meaning "fleshy," and the suffix "-osis," indicating "condition." Here's a brief history:

- 3.6 Million Years Ago: Sarcoidosis claims its first victim among Australopithecus ancestors.
- 2,353 B.C.: The first-ever sarcoidosis biopsy occurs during a Bronze Age altercation.
- 501 A.D.: Theodoric Dung, a sufferer, keeps his enlightenment discovery to himself due to illness.
- 1287: Coughing becomes fashionable at King Henrik's court, possibly indicating sarcoidosis.
- 1877: Dr. Hutchinson jokes about sarcoidosis, attributing symptoms to imagination.
- 1889: Dr. Cesar Boeck coins "multiple benign sarcoid of the skin."
- 1920: Sarcoidosis becomes official, derived from 'Sarc,' 'Oid,' and 'Osis.'
- 1941: World War II drafting leads to increased sarcoidosis diagnoses.
- 1958: The first sarcoidosis conference ends in laughter and cigars.

- 1965: Prednisone's availability leads to widespread prescriptions.
- 1972: Susan 'moonchild' Coombs explores holistic approaches to sarcoidosis.
- 1977: Limited Edition Prednisone Packs commemorate 100 years of medical ignorance.
- 1996: Internet connectivity allows sarcoidosis sufferers to connect and share experiences.
- 2002: The World Consortium on Sarcoidosis Research claims sarcoidosis goes into remission.
- 2007: Sarcoidosis research receives government funding between peculiar research projects.

Sarcoidosis in India

Despite a brief review of sarcoidosis, accompanied by a case report, being published as early as 1957 in the Indian Journal of Dermatology, the disease remained largely obscured by the prevailing tuberculosis epidemic for an extended period. It wasn't until the late S. Gupta began disseminating his insights into the clinical aspects of sarcoidosis in India, sharing his experiences at numerous national and international conferences. In Kolkata, India, on February 22, 2003, the Indian Association of Sarcoidosis and other Granulomatous Disorders (IASOG) was formally established. Tragically, these developments occurred after the passing of S. Gupta, a trailblazer in the fields of sarcoidosis and tuberculosis, who had already succumbed to illness on September 9, 2002. The pioneers of sarcoidosis include several great masters worldwide. Some of them are mentioned here.

CHAPTER THREE

PIONEERS OF SARCOIDOSIS

Jonathan Hutchinson: Identified the first case of sarcoidosis at King's College Hospital, London, over a century ago. He described multiple raised, dusty-red patches on the patient's feet, fingers, and arms.

Jonathon Hutchinson

The first patient with sarcoidosis described by J. Hutchinson had multiple, raised, dusty-red patches on his feet, fingers and arms

Robert Willan: Introduced the term "erythema nodosum" and made significant contributions to modern dermatology.

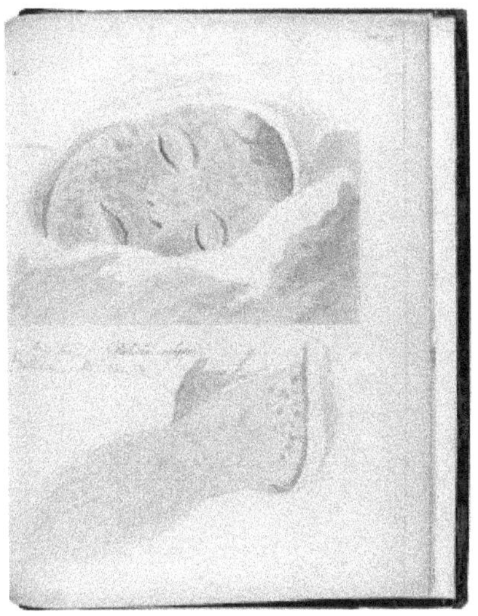

Erythema nodosum

Ernst Henri Besnier: First to report lupus pernio and introduced the term "biopsy."

Ernst Henry Besnier

Caesar Peter Moller Boeck: Described skin lesions in a patient with lymphadenopathy as "lymphoma cutis multiplex/multiple benign sarcoids of the skin."

Cesar Peter Moller Boeck

Jorgen Schaumann: First to report systemic sarcoidosis, calling it "lymphogranulomatosis benigna."

Jogren Schaumann

Sven Löfgren: Linked erythema nodosum with sarcoidosis, known as "Löfgren's syndrome.

Sven Lofgren

Louis Eliot Siltzbach: Established the diagnostic value of the Kveim test, now known as the Kveim Siltzbach test.

Louis Eliot Siltzbach

Carol Johnson Johns: Organized the first International Conference on Sarcoidosis in 1984.

Carol Johnson Johns

Keitzo Nobechi: Reported the uneven geographic distribution of Japanese cases of sarcoidosis.

Keitzo Nobechi

Om P Sharma: Contributed to raising awareness of sarcoidosis in India through the Indian Association of Sarcoidosis and other Granulomatous Disorders (IASOG).

Enter Om P Sharma

Sarcoidosis Milestones:

1869: J. Hutchinson's first account of skin lesions

1888: E. Besnier coins term lupus pernio

1892: M. Tenneson defines histology

1897: C. Boeck describes a policeman with skin lesions

1902: R. Kienbock/K. Kreibich/O. Jungling describes bone changes

1906: Darier–Roussy syndrome: subcutaneous nodules described

1909–1910: H. Schumacher/Christian Heerfordt/F. Bering recognize uveitis

1915: J. Schaumann emphasizes multisystemic disorder

1915: E. Kuznitsky classifies skin lesions

1915: A. Bittorf describes lung lesions

1937: W. Bruins-Slot/L-M. Pautrier/W.T. Longcope/J. Pierson/ J. Costa Waldenstrom describe uveoparotid fever

1941: A. Kveim introduces the Kveim test S. Lofgren describes Lofgren's syndrome

1958: K. Wurm proposes the first radiographic staging

1958: 1st International Conference on Sarcoidosis: London

1961: 1st USA conference: Washington, DC, USA

1967–1981: H. Reynolds, G. Hunninghake, R Crystal pioneer bronchoalveolar lavage

1976: Commemorative publication dedicated to L. Siltzbach: Mount Sinai Journal of Medicine, New York

1984: G. Rizzato starts the journal Sarcoidosis (now called Sarcoidosis, Vasculitis, and Diffuse Lung Diseases)

1987: G. Rizzato founds World Association of Sarcoidosis and Other Granulomatous Disorders (WASOG); D.G. James elected the first president

1987: First commemorative publication dedicated to D.G. James: Sarcoidosis

CHAPTER FOUR

STUDIES RELATED TO HOMOEOPATHY

Introduction

The word 'Homoeopathy' is derived from two Greek words, 'Homois'- meaning similar, and 'pathos'- meaning suffering. Homoeopathy simply means treating diseases with remedies, prescribed in minute doses, which are capable of producing symptoms similar to the disease when taken by healthy people. It is based on the natural law of healing- "Similia Similibus Curantur" which means "likes cure likes". Dr. Christian Friedrich Samuel Gottfried Hahnemann gave it a scientific basis in the early 19th century. It has been serving suffering humanity for over two centuries and has withstood the upheavals of time and has emerged as a time-tested therapy. The scientific principles propounded by Dr. Hahnemann are natural and well-proven and continue to be followed with success.

Current Scenario

Homoeopathy today is a rapidly growing system and is being practiced almost all over the world. In India, it has become a household name due to the safety of its pills and the gentleness of its cure. A rough study indicates that about 10% of the Indian population solely depends on Homoeopathy for their healthcare needs. It has blended so well into the roots and traditions of the country that it has been recognized as one of the National Systems of Medicine and plays an important role in providing health care to a large number of people.

Origin of Homoeopathy

The principle of Homoeopathy has been known since the time of Hippocrates from Greece, the founder of medicine, around 450 BC. More than a thousand years later, the Swiss alchemist Paracelsus employed the same system of healing based upon the principle that "like cures like". But it was not until the late 18th century that Homoeopathy as it is practiced today was evolved by the great German physician, Dr. Samuel Hahnemann. He was appalled by the medical practices of that time and set about to develop a method of healing that would be safe, gentle, and effective.

Discovery by Hahnemann

Over two hundred years ago, the German physician Dr. Samuel Hahnemann discovered the principle that whatever substance could cause in the way of symptoms, it could also cure. Dr. Hahnemann was struck by the effect that certain drugs when taken by him while quite healthy, produced symptoms that the drug was known to cure in sick. For instance, when he took Cinchona Bark, which contains quinine, he became ill with symptoms that exactly mimicked intermittent fever (now called malaria). He wondered if the reason Cinchona worked against intermittent fever was because it caused symptoms indistinguishable from intermittent fever in a healthy human as demonstrated by Dr. William Cullen in his Materia Medica.

Hahnemann caught the essence of this action of cinchona while translating the works of Dr. Cullen in 1789 giving birth to the true and the only system of medicine based on nature's law of cure, treating a person as a whole, not its parts or organs, therefore also called as the holistic system of treatment.

Experimental Approach

Master Hahnemann continued to experiment, noting that every substance he took, whether an herb, a mineral, an animal product, or a chemical compound, produced definite distinct symptoms in him.

He further noted that no two substances produced the same set of symptoms. Each provoked its unique pattern of symptoms. Furthermore, the symptoms were not just confined to the physical plane. Every substance tested also affected the mind and the emotions apart from the body. Eventually, Dr. Hahnemann began to treat the sick on the principle of 'let likes be treated by likes'. From the outset, he achieved outstanding clinical success.

Dr. William Cullen, Pharmaceutical Bottle of Quinine used by Hahnemann and Front Page of Cullen's Materia Medica

however, well known to physicians, that the most considerable instance of the sympathy mentioned above, is afforded by the stomach, so connected with almost every other part of the system, that motions excited there are communicated to almost every other part of the body, and produce peculiar effects in those parts, however distant from the stomach itself. This indeed is very well known; but that the effects of many medicines which appear in other parts of the body are entirely owing to an action upon the stomach, and that the most part of medicines acting upon the system act immediately upon the stomach only, is what has not been understood till very lately, and does not seem even yet to be very generally and fully perceived by the writers on the materia medica. It will, therefore, be proper here to say in what manner this doctrine may be established.

"*First :* That medicines shewing considerable powers with respect to the whole system, act especially or only on the stomach, will appear from all those cases in which the effects appear soon after the substance has been taken into the stomach, and before they can be supposed to have gone further into the body, or to have reached the mass of blood. Thus, Sir John Pringle, from the sudden operation of the Peruvian bark in preventing the paroxysms of intermittent fevers, properly concludes, that it cannot be by its antiseptic powers with respect to the fluids, but by a certain operation immediately upon the stomach. (See Diseases of the Army, Appendix, p. xxv.)

"*Secondly :* As medicines are commonly in the first place applied to the stomach, so all those of volatile, active, and penetrating parts, must immediately and especially act upon the stomach; and from this consideration, as well as from the suddenness of their effects which commonly appear, we may conclude their action to be upon the stomach only. Accordingly, I conclude that the action of the volatile alkali, and some other saline substances, is upon the stomach alone, and very rarely by any antiseptic powers with respect to the fluids.

"*Thirdly :* Though medicines do not to the taste or smell discover any volatile or active parts, yet if their effects depend upon the change which they produce in the state of the nervous power, it is hardly to be doubted that they operate only

Page No. 151 of Cullen's Materia Medica showing Cinchona Pharmacology- Adopted from The Works of William Cullen by John Thomson- Edinburgh

Hahnemann divided sickness into-

1. **Indisposition**- slight alteration in the state of health manifested by one or more trivial symptoms. Slight alteration in diet or/and regimen will dispel it.
2. **Surgical diseases**- the diseases with gross pathological, often irreversible changes.
3. **Dynamic diseases**- the diseases due to functional derangement of normal harmony of health, often reversible.

A. **Acute Diseases**- any disease or illness that can disturb the health of a person temporarily in a negative way. They are rapid in course, intense in pain and severity, short or moderate in duration, and end in recovery or death.

   a. **Individual**- occurring only in one individual at a time with different groups of symptoms.
   b. **Sporadic**- attacking several persons at a time in different localities with somewhat similar symptoms. viz. Viral Fever, Influenza, Dysentery, Typhoid etc.
   c. **Endemic**- diseases prevalent in a particular locality due to some local circumstances.
   d. **Epidemic**- attacking a large number of persons in a vast area at a time with a similar set of symptoms.

      i. **Immunizing**- occurs only once in the lifetime of an individual, profylacting against a second attack. viz. Smallpox, Chicken pox, Measles, Whooping Cough, Scarlet Fever, Mumps, etc..
      ii. **Nonimmunizing**- may occur several times in the life of an individual. viz. Cholera, Plague, Yellow Fever, Diphtheria etc.

e. **Pandemic**- attacking a large area of the world with similar symptoms. viz. influenza.

B. **Chronic diseases**- the diseases appearing insidiously, running indefinitely, and leaving lifelong consequences or terminating in death, often based on activities of one or more means, the fundamental causes of all chronic diseases.

a. **Artificial**- iatrogenic diseases. i.e. diseases due to excessive use of drugs.
b. **Inappropriately named chronic diseases**- false chronic diseases, persisting due to some maintaining cause. viz. occupational diseases; bad habits, dust exposure, etc.
c. **True Natural or Miasmatic diseases**- chronic diseases with constitutional signs and symptoms.

i. **One-sided diseases**- having very few perceptive symptoms.

- **Internal**- affection of an internal kind, viz. chronic headache or diarrhea.
- **External**- affection of an external kind localized in one part only, viz. venous stasis, varicose veins, etc.

i. **Diseases with fully developed symptoms**- these are full-fledged chronic diseases.

a. **Single diseases**- having only one miasm at a time.

- **Psora**- the functional miasm causing disturbances in physiology only.
- **Sycosis**- the mal-growth miasm, causing exfoliations, tumorization etc.
- **Syphilis**- the degenerating miasm, causing destructions.

a. **Compound Diseases**- diseases having the combination of more than one miasm.

- **Psora-sycosis**- abnormal growths. viz. tumors, keloids, etc.
- **Psora-syphilis**- also called Pseudopsora, or Tubercular miasm, causing tubercular degenerations, etc. viz. phthisis.
- **Syco-syphilis**- causing cystic degeneration. viz. Tubo-ovarian mass etc.
- **Psora-syco-syphilis**- also called cancerous miasm, causes the worst forms of diseases like cancer.

CHAPTER FIVE

SARCOIDOSIS, A COMPREHENSIVE STUDY

Definition of Sarcoidosis-

It is hard to provide a concise definition of a disease whose cause is yet to be discovered. Scadding and Mitchell recommended the following: "Sarcoidosis is a disease characterized by the formation in all of several affected tissues of epithelioid-cell tubercles without caseation though fibrinoid necrosis may be present at the center of a few, proceeding either to resolution or to conversion into hyaline fibrous tissue".

Other Definitions of Sarcoidosis-

- A systemic granulomatous disease of unknown cause, especially involving the lungs with resulting fibrosis, but also involving lymph nodes, skin, liver, spleen, eyes, phalangeal bones, and parotid glands; granulomas are composed of epithelioid and multinucleated giant cells with little or no necrosis. Syn: Besnier-Boeck-Schaumann disease, Besnier-Boeck-Schaumann syndrome, Boeck's disease, Boeck's sarcoid, Schaumann's syndrome.

- ○ X Term Medical Dictionary

- A systemic granulomatous disease of unknown cause, especially involving the lungs with resulting fibrosis, but also involving lymph nodes, skin, liver, spleen, eyes, phalangeal bones, and parotid glands; granulomas are composed of epithelioid and multinucleated giant cells with little or no necrosis. Syn: Besnier-Boeck-Schaumann disease, Besnier-Boeck-Schaumann syndrome, Boeck's disease, Boeck's sarcoid, sarcoid(1), Schaumann's syndrome.

  - ○ Stedman's Electronic Medical Dictionary V. 4.0

- A chronic disease of unknown cause marked by the formation of nodules in the lungs and liver and lymph glands and salivary glands.

  - ○ wordnetweb.princeton.edu/perl/webwn

- Sarcoidosis (sarc = flesh, -oid = like, -osis = a process), also called sarcoid or Besnier-Boeck disease, is a multisystem disorder characterized by non-caseating granulomas (small inflammatory nodules). The cause of the disease is still unknown.

  - ○ en.wikipedia.org/wiki/Sarcoidosis

- A rare inflammation of the lymph nodes and other tissues throughout the body. sella turcica - bony structure that houses the pituitary gland. suprarenal glands - another name for the adrenal glands.

  - ○ www.methodisthealth.com/tmhs/basic.do

- A systemic disease involving the lungs, lymph nodes, skin, liver, spleen, eyes, phalangial bones, and parotid glands, characterized by granular nodules. Its cause is not known.

- ◦ www.cdc.gov/cfs/cfsglossary.htm

- A condition that causes small, fleshy swellings in the liver, lungs, and spleen.

  - ◦ ukhealthcare.uky.edu/patient/glossary/glossary-s.htm

- A disease of unknown origin that causes small lumps (granulomas) due to chronic inflammation to develop in a great range of body tissues. Sarcoidosis can appear in almost any body organ, but most often starts in the lungs or lymph nodes.

  - ◦ www.emedicinehealth.com/arthritis/glossary_em.htm

- A chronic, progressive, systemic granulomatous reticulosis of unknown etiology, involving almost any organ or tissue, including the skin, lungs.

  - ◦ courses.washington.edu/hubio567/lang/term2.html

- An inflammatory disease marked by the formation of granulomas (small nodules of immune cells) in the lungs, lymph nodes, and other organs.

  - ◦ www.ecancerawareness.com/cancer_glossary/s.php

- A rare disease with no known cause that leads to inflammation in tissues throughout the body, including the lymph nodes, lungs, liver, skin, and eyes.

  - ◦ www.american-depot.com/services/resources_gl_s.asp

- Sarcoidosis is a multi system disorder characterized in affected organs by a type of inflammation called granulomas. The cause is unknown. Some people with sarcoidosis affecting their pituitary glands can develop diabetes insipidus.

  - www.diabetesinsipidus.org/whatisdi_glossary.htm

- A rheumatic disease that often involves a sudden onset of arthritis in the feet and ankles.

  - www.arthritis.org/disease-center.php

- An inflammatory disease that can affect almost any organ in the body. It causes heightened immunity which means that a person's immune system, which normally protects the body from infection and disease, overreacts, resulting in damage to the body's own tissues.

  - www.stopsarcoidosis.org/sarcoidosis/glossary.htm

- A disease characterized by granulomas (small growths of blood vessels, cells, and connective tissue) that can lead to problems in the skin, lungs, eyes, joints, and muscles.

  - womenshealth.about.com/library/bl_autoimmune12.htm

- Some doctors use melatonin to help treat sarcoidosis (a condition where fibrous tissue develops in the lungs and other tissues). A few clinical studies suggest that melatonin may be helpful for those who do not improve from conventional steroid treatment.

  - dukehealthsystem.adam.com/content.aspx

Sarcoidosis - Synonyms

Sarcoidosis is also known as:

1. Besnier-Boeck-Schaumann disease
2. Schaumann's syndrome
3. Schaumann-Besnier syndrome
4. Besnier-Boeck disease
5. Besnier-Boeck-Schaumann-Schaumann's syndrome

Incidence and Prevalence

Geographical Incidence

Europe: The prevalence ranges from 3-50 cases per 100,000 population, with the disease most frequently affecting persons aged 20-40 years.

Sweden: Reported as the highest incidence in Europe, ranging from 64 to 641 cases per 100,000 population.

United Kingdom: The overall prevalence of sarcoidosis is approximately 20 per 100,000 population.

Denmark: Approximate incidence in Danish children younger than 15 years is 0.22-0.27 per 100,000 children per year.

New York: 39 out of every 100,000 are affected.

Spain: Only 1.2 per 100,000 are infected.

Rare Occurrences: Sarcoidosis is rarely reported in the Middle East, China, SE Asia, or among the Inuit or Native North Americans.

Portugal, India, Saudi Arabia, or South America: Prevalence is low, possibly due to the absence of mass chest radiographic screening and the presence of other more commonly recognized granulomatous diseases, especially tuberculosis.

Racial Incidence

Within a geographical area, the frequency and course of the disease vary considerably among racial groups. For instance:

- In London, the incidence among W. Indian and Asian immigrants is 10 times higher than in the indigenous Caucasian population.
- In South Africa, sarcoidosis occurs in 23 out of every 100,000 black persons, 12 of every 100,000 mixed-race persons, and 4 of every 100,000 Caucasians.
- In the United States, African Americans are more affected compared to Caucasians.

Genetic Factorial Incidence

- Prevalence in certain races
- Familial clustering
- HLA genetic factors play a role.

Sexual Incidence

African American women develop sarcoidosis twice as often as African American men, while Caucasian women and men are equally likely to develop it. Overall, it is more frequent in females.

Age Incidence

The highest prevalence is in 25-34 year olds.

Smokers vs. Nonsmokers Incidence

Contrary to most lung diseases, sarcoidosis occurs more frequently in nonsmokers than smokers.

Characteristic Features of Sarcoidosis

- Often symptomless
- May present with chest discomfort, malaise, fever
- Can progress to dyspnea, cor pulmonale, death
- Honeycomb appearance on chest x-ray
- Restrictive pattern on PFTs

Common Symptoms of Sarcoidosis

Sarcoidosis, a complex multisystem disease, manifests in various ways, often affecting multiple organs. Here are the common symptoms:

General Symptoms:

- General discomfort, uneasiness, or malaise
- Fever
- Shortness of breath
- Persistent cough
- Skin lesions or rashes
- Headaches
- Visual changes
- Neurological changes
- Enlarged lymph glands
- Enlarged liver and spleen, leading to decreased platelets and abdominal pain
- Dry mouth
- Fatigue and weight loss

Additional Symptoms:

- Tearing, decreased
- Seizures
- Nosebleeds
- Joint stiffness and pain
- Hair loss
- Eye burning, itching, and discharge
- Abnormal breath sounds
- Nasal obstruction or frequent sinusitis

Organ-Specific Symptoms:

Lung Symptoms:

- Shortness of breath
- Dry cough
- Wheezing
- Chest pain (rare)

Lymph Node Symptoms:

- Enlarged and sometimes tender lymph nodes, commonly in the neck and chest

Skin Symptoms:

- Various types of bumps, ulcers, or discolored areas
- Painful bumps called erythema nodosum
- Disfiguring skin sores, known as lupus pernio

Eye Symptoms:

- Burning, itching, tearing
- Redness
- Sensitivity to light
- Dryness
- Blurred vision

Heart Symptoms:

- Shortness of breath
- Leg swelling
- Coughing
- Irregular heartbeat
- Sudden loss of consciousness

Joint and Muscle Symptoms:

- Joint stiffness, swelling, and pain
- Muscle pain or weakness
- Arthritis in ankles
- Bone symptoms, including painless holes or swelling

Liver Symptoms:

- Fever
- Fatigue
- Itching
- Abdominal pain
- Enlarged liver

Gland Symptoms:

- Swelling, especially in cheeks
- Dryness in mouth and throat

Blood, Urinary Tract, and Kidney Symptoms:

- Increased calcium levels
- Confusion
- Increased urination

Nervous System Symptoms:

- Headaches
- Vision problems
- Weakness or numbness
- Facial drooping
- Paralysis
- Sensory changes

Pituitary Gland Symptoms (Rare):

- Headaches
- Vision problems
- Weakness or numbness
- Coma

Clinical Staging of Sarcoidosis

Although most cases of sarcoidosis either regress or remain stable, 10-15% progress to pulmonary fibrosis. Generally, pulmonary function worsens with an increasing stage of the disease, but radiologic staging does not correlate well with the severity of pulmonary function abnormalities. Often, the radiographic abnormalities appear worse than the degree of functional impairment present.

This is based on the pattern of chest radiographic findings-

Radiographic staging of Sarcoidosis				
Stage	Hilar adenopathy	Parenchymal disease	Percent at onset	Percent with resolution
0	No	No	<10	NA
1	Yes	No	50	65
2	Yes	Yes	30	20-50
3	No	Yes	10-15	<20
4	No	w/ fibrosis	10-15	<20

Radiographic staging of Sarcoidosis

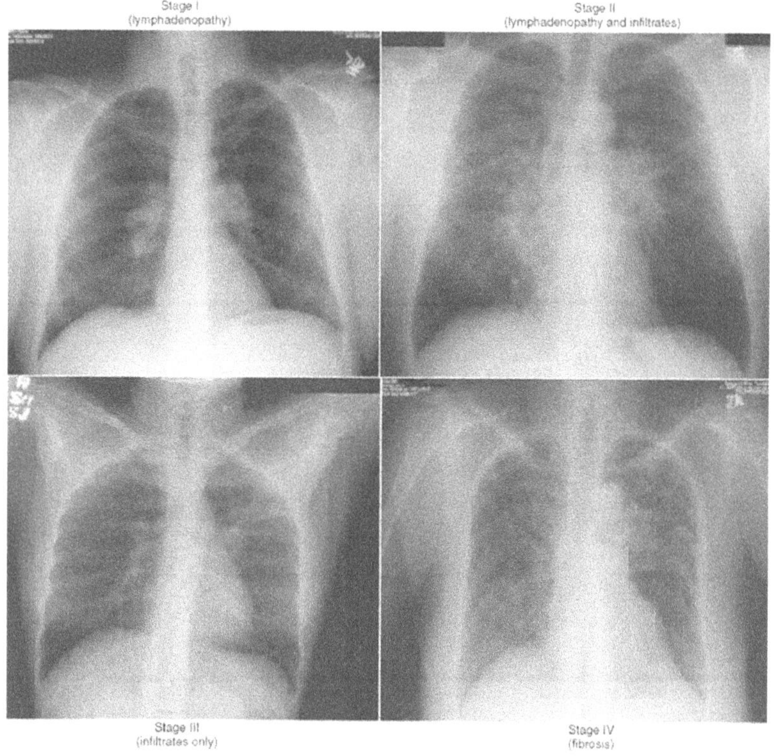

Chest radiographs PA view

Stage 0	a normal chest radiograph
Stage I	lymphadenopathy only
Stage II	lymphadenopathy and lung parenchymal disease
Stage III	parenchymal lung disease only
Stage IV	pulmonary fibrosis

Frequency of organ involvement

The frequency of organ involvement varies considerably. The organ involvement rates may be as follows-

Organ	Prevalance
Lung	90%
Lymph nodes	75-90%
Pleura	01-05%
Skin	25%
Eye	25%
Nasal mucosa	20%
Larynx	05%
Bone marrow	15-40%
Spleen	50-60%
Liver	60-90%
Kidney	Rare
Calcium disorder	01-02%
CNS	05%
Bones	05%
Joints	25-50%
Heart	05%
Endocrine glands	Rare
Parotid gland	10%
GI tract	Rare

Frequency of organ involvement

EXPLORING SARCOIDOSIS: UNRAVELING POTENTIAL TRIGGERS

Infectious Agents:

1. Mycobacteria:

- **Tuberculous:** Mycobacterium tuberculosis, associated with tuberculosis.
- **Nontuberculous:** Other Mycobacterium species apart from tuberculosis.
- **Cell-wall Deficient (L-forms):** Mycobacterial forms lack cell walls, posing diagnostic challenges.

2. Bacteria:

- **Corynebacterium spp.:** Corynebacterium species with possible involvement.
- **Propionibacterium acnes:** Known for acne association but also suspected in sarcoidosis.

- **Tropheryma whippleii:** Bacterium linked to Whipple's disease, a rare disorder affecting multiple systems.

3. Fungi:

- **Cryptococcus spp.:** Fungal species, including Cryptococcus neoformans, under scrutiny.
- **Endemic Fungi:** Fungal strains prevalent in specific regions, potentially playing a role.

4. Viruses:

- **Cytomegalovirus:** Herpesvirus implicated in various diseases.
- **Epstein-Barr Virus:** Common herpesvirus associated with infectious mononucleosis.
- **Herpes Simplex Virus:** Known for causing oral and genital herpes infections.
- **Others:** Various viral agents under investigation for their possible contribution.

Noninfectious Triggers:

1. Dusts:

- **Clay, Pine, Pollen, Talc:** Particulate matter from diverse sources possibly linked to sarcoidosis.
- **Mixed Dust Exposure:** Combination of different dust types presenting potential risk factors.

2. Metals:

- **Aluminum, Beryllium, Zirconium:** Metals with industrial and environmental presence speculated to trigger immune responses.

Pathophysiology

Exploring the intricate interplay between these suspected causes and the immune system offers insights into the complex pathophysiology of sarcoidosis. Further research aims to elucidate the precise mechanisms underlying disease development and progression.

1. **Interaction of Antigens:**

    - Alveolar macrophages with increased MHC class II molecule expression interact with unknown antigens.
    - Activated T-lymphocytes (Th-1) release cytokines like interleukin-2, monocyte chemotactic factor, and others.

2. **Granuloma Formation:**

    - Interleukin-2 activates T lymphocytes, while monocyte chemotactic factor attracts monocytes.
    - Macrophage migration inhibitory factor influences monocytes to transform into epithelioid cells and form granulomas.

3. **Lung Injury:**

    - Granuloma formation and alveolitis by CD4+ T-lymphocytes can lead to lung injury.
    - Peripheral blood shows CD4+ T-lymphopenia and depressed cutaneous delayed hypersensitivity.

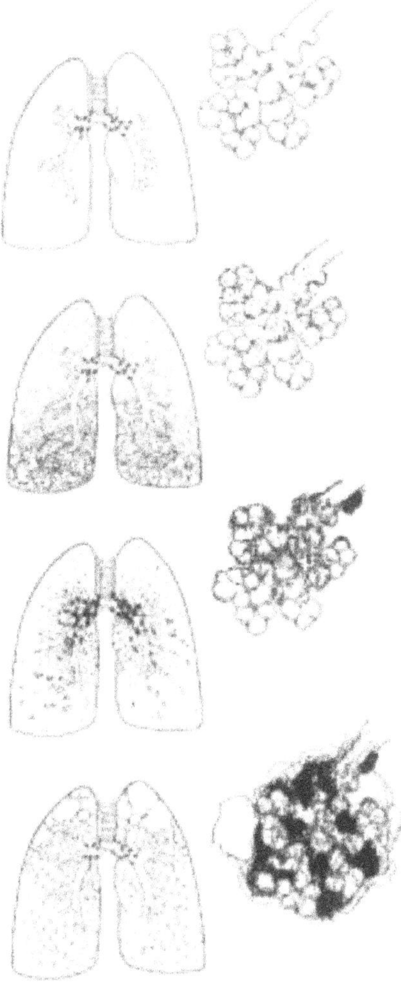

Inflammatory phases in lung Sarcoidosis. Magnified view shows how illness may affect the normal lung, going from alveolitis to granuloma formation, to fibrosis

1. **Circulating Immune Complexes:**

- ○ B-cell function increases, leading to hyperglobulinemia and the presence of circulating immune complexes.

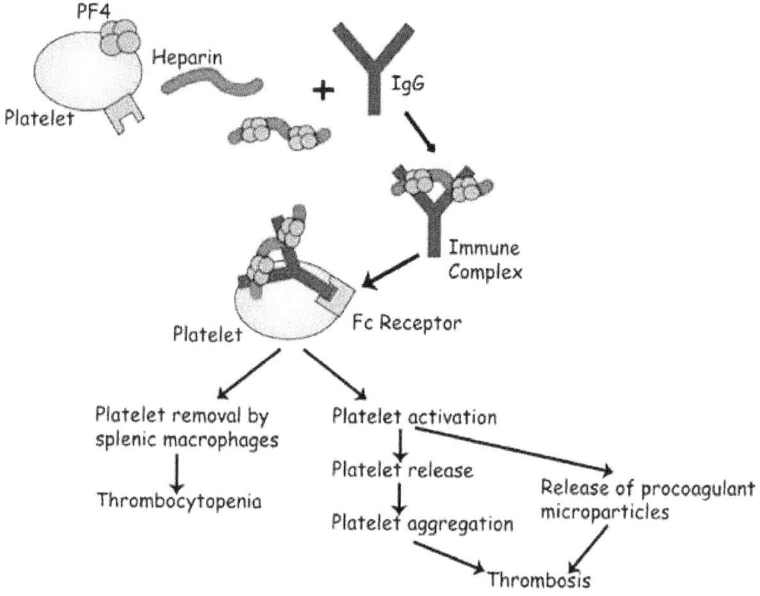

Circulating immune complexes

1. Fibrosis:

- ○ Activated macrophages release fibronectin, cytokines, and growth factors, contributing to fibrosis.

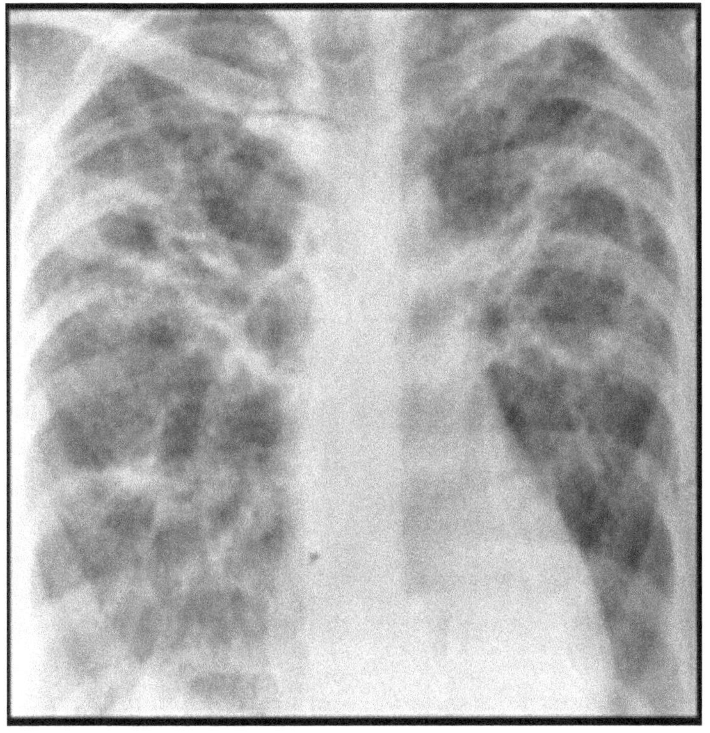

Extensive lung fibrosis

CHAPTER SEVEN

EXPLORING SARCOIDOSIS: CLINICAL IMPLICATIONS

Clinical Implications:

- **Inflammatory Phases:** The immunological cascade causes tissue changes, granuloma formation, immune complex presence, B-cell hyperactivity, and depression of hypersensitivity reactions.
- **Lung Fibrosis:** Extensive fibrosis may occur due to the release of mediators by activated macrophages.

Gender Differences:

- **Female Predominance:** Sarcoidosis is slightly more common in women than in men.
- **Oxidative Stress:** Chronic inflammation leads to oxidative stress, contributing to telomere erosion in blood cells.
- **Hormonal Influence:** Estrogen-induced vascular endothelial growth factor expression may aggravate inflammation and

oxidative stress. However, estrogen might also have a protective effect by stimulating telomerase and reducing oxidative stress.

- **Telomere Shortening:** Female sarcoidosis patients show significant telomere shortening compared to males, suggesting a weaker protective function of estrogen in sarcoidosis.

Manifestations and Associations

1. **General Manifestations:**

   - Fever, anorexia, weight loss, lymphadenopathy, parotid enlargement, acute arthritis, nasal stuffiness, hoarseness, etc.

2. **Pulmonary Manifestations:**

   - Dyspnea, dry cough, and chest pain are common.
   - Involvement of parenchyma, lymph nodes, and airways.
   - Uncommon manifestations include pleural effusion, pneumothorax, cavity formation, and more.

3. **Otorhinolaryngological Manifestations:**

   - Parotid enlargement, hoarseness, nasal stuffiness.

4. **Dermatological Manifestations:**

   - Lesions such as erythema nodosum, maculopapular rash, scars, keloids, plaques, papules, and subcutaneous nodules.
   - Lupus pernio, onycholysis, nasal and conjunctival mucosal granulomas are other presentations.

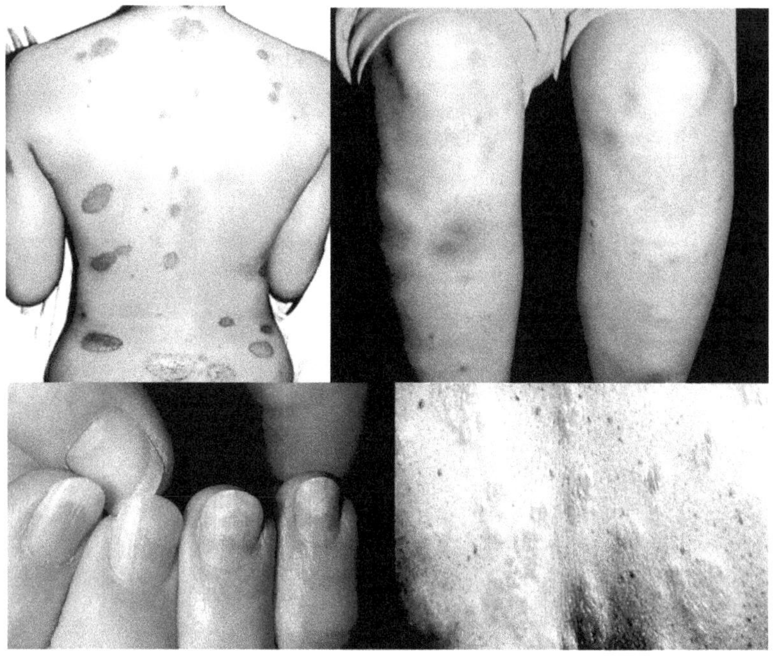

Erythema nodosum and onycholysis

1. **Cardiological Manifestations:**

    ◦ Dyspnea, cardiac failure, arrhythmias, conduction abnormalities, abnormal ECG, cough, wheezing, cor pulmonale, valvular involvement, and more.
    ◦ Myocardial infarction-like picture with myocardial involvement.

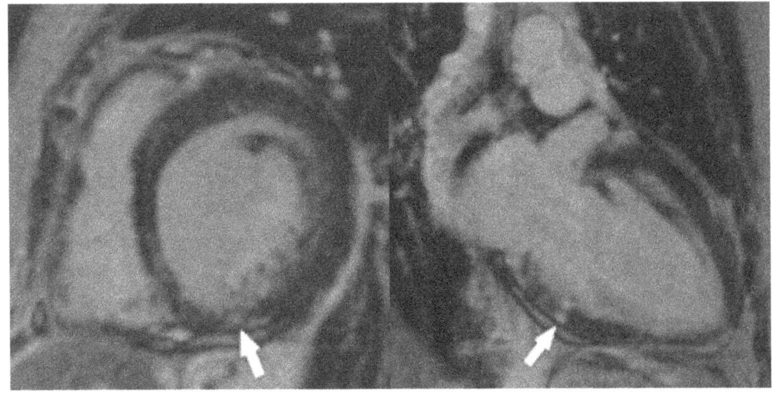

Cardiac MRI- location (subendocardial, transmural, subepicardial, or mesocardial) & pattern (patchy or diffuse) of abnormal delayed myocardial enhancement allows differentiation between ischemic and nonischemic cardiomyopathies

6. Nephrological Manifestations:

- Renal failure risk with findings like glomerulosclerosis, glomerulonephritis, and hypercalciuria.

7. Radiological Manifestations:

- Abnnormal chest X-ray, bilateral hilar lymphadenopathy, and interstitial fibrosis.

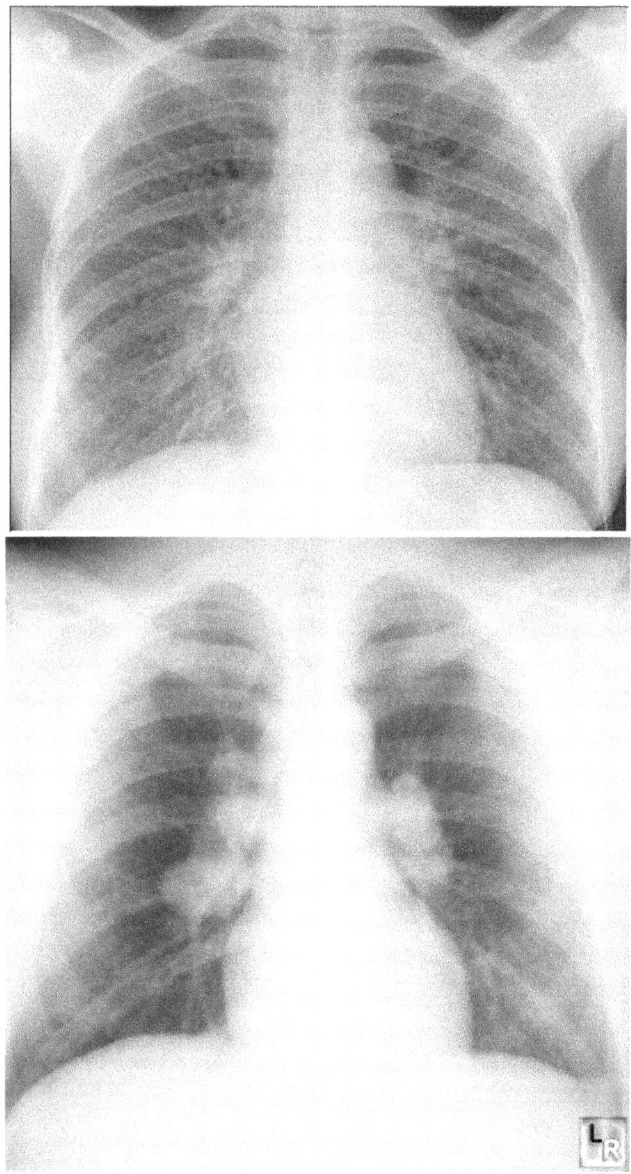

Chest PA - bilateral hilar adenopathy with "separation" of nodes
from the heart (broncho-pulmonary nodes in sarcoid are more

peripherally placed than true hilar nodes that enlarge in lymphoma)

8. Hepatological Manifestations:

- Portal hypertension, abnormal liver function tests, and hepatomegaly in rare cases.

9. Mammary Gland Manifestations:

- Rare involvement, presenting as palpable masses or nodular densities on mammography.

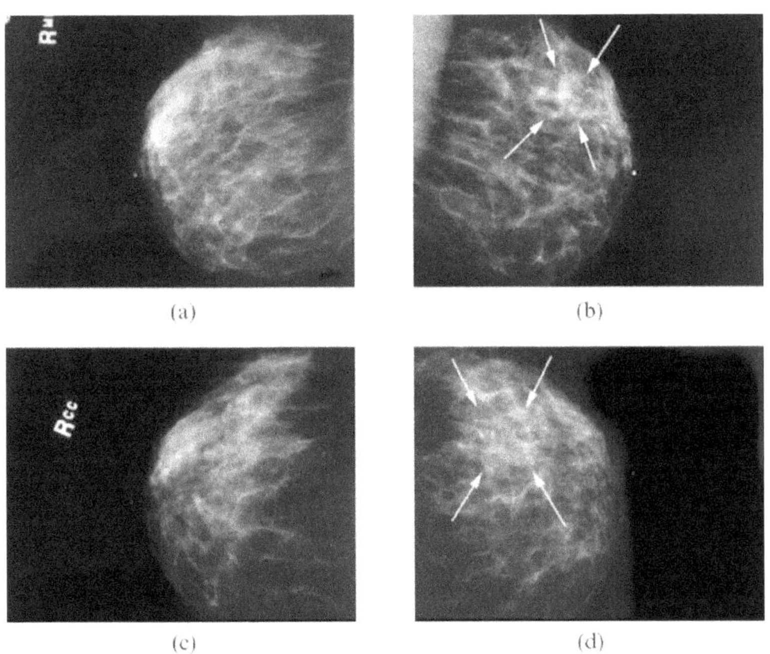

(a)   (b)

(c)   (d)

(a,b) Mediolateral oblique and (c,d) craniocaudal views of both breasts demonstrate an asymmetric density in the upper outer quadrant of the left breast (a,c)

10. **Lymphatic System Manifestations:**

   - Involvement of cervical, epitrochlear, axillary, and inguinal nodes, usually non-ulcerative and discrete.

11. **Rheumatological Manifestations:**

   - Arthritis and bone cysts are observed.

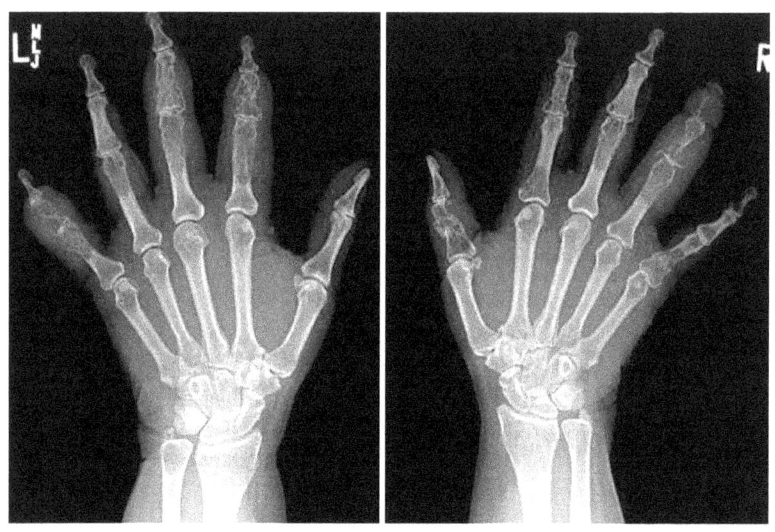

Diffuse trabecular change, leads to a latticework or lacy network configuration, and multiple lucent lesions of varying sizes are found in the fingers. (The lytic change produces a cystic-like appearance)

12. **Endocrinological Manifestations:**

- ◦ Rare occurrences include diabetes insipidus, hypercalcemia, and hyperthyroidism.

13. Ophthalmological Manifestations:

- ◦ Conjunctivitis, iritis, uveitis, choroiditis, and various eye-related symptoms.

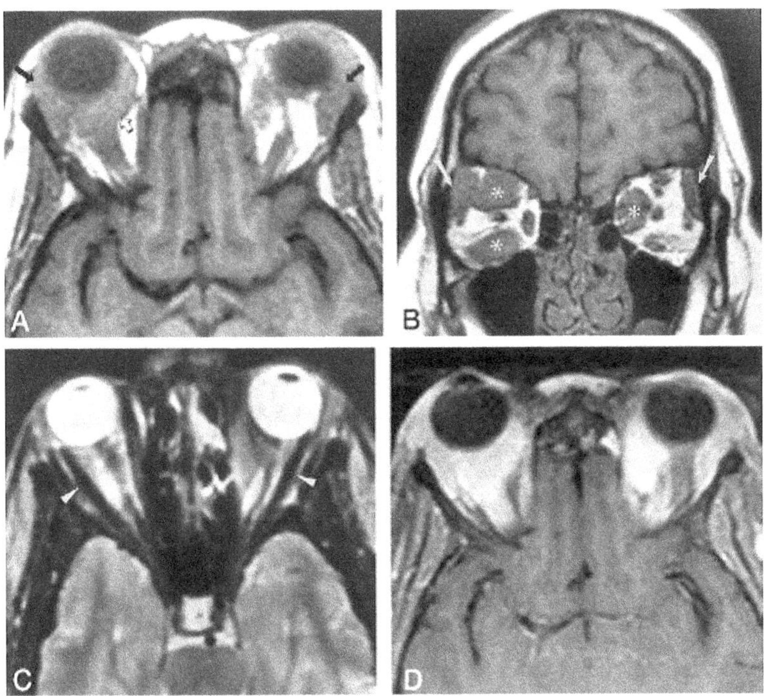

MRI of a 43-year-old woman with horizontal and vertical diplopia. A–D, Axial (A) and coronal (B) T1- weighted images through the orbits show marked enlargement of the lachrymal glands (solid arrows) and rectus muscles (asterisks) as well as the markedly enlarged insertion of the right superior rectus muscle (open arrow). Axial T2-weighted image (C) shows markedly hypointense rectus muscles (arrowheads). Axial contrast-enhanced T1-weighted fat-suppressed image (D) shows intense abnormal enhancement of the lacrimal glands and extraocular muscles

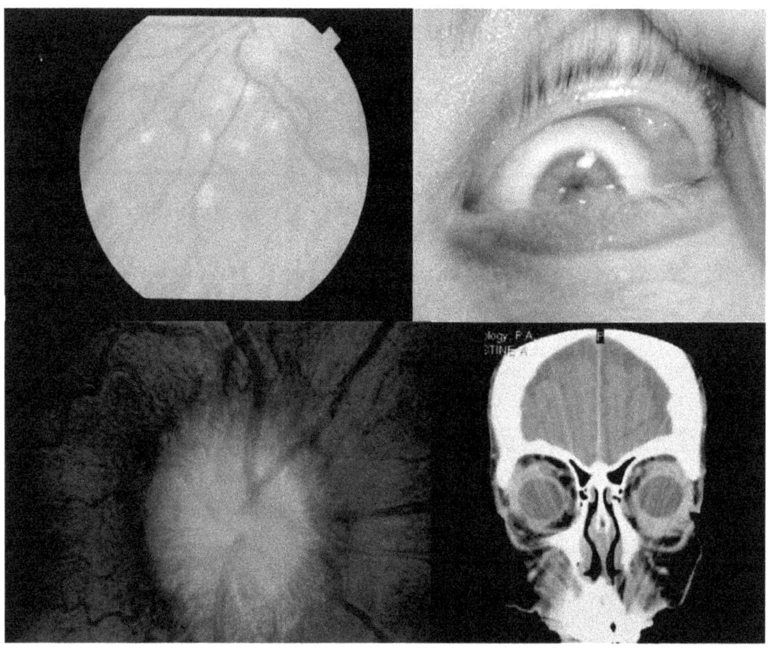

Sarcoidosis can result in anterior uveitis, granuloma in the eyes (red, swollen palpebral lobe of the lachrymal gland is observed on eversion of the upper eyelids), and/or enlarged lachrymal and salivary glands (Mikulicz syndrome)

14. **Urological Manifestations:**

   ○ Hypercalciuria is a notable finding.

15. **Sarcoidosis and Malignancy:**

- Adenocarcinoma is the most associated cancer type, with sarcoid-like reactions observed in regional lymph nodes.

16. **Sarcoidosis and Pregnancy:**

- Pregnancy-associated hormonal changes can impact sarcoidosis activity, with potential exacerbation postpartum.

17. **Neurological Manifestations:**

- Cranial nerve palsies, seizures, peripheral neuropathy, and more.

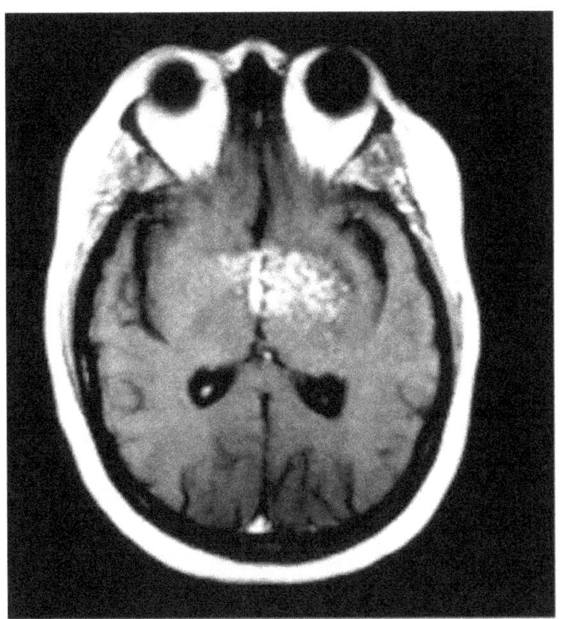

CT Head- 1.5 cm enhancing suprasellar cistern mass lifting the optic chiasm slightly in the cephalad direction

18. Myological Manifestations:

- Granulomatous muscle involvement, myopathy, and polymyositis may be observed.

19. Orthopaedic Manifestations:

- Lytic lesions, periosteal reaction, digital clubbing, and involvement of various bones.

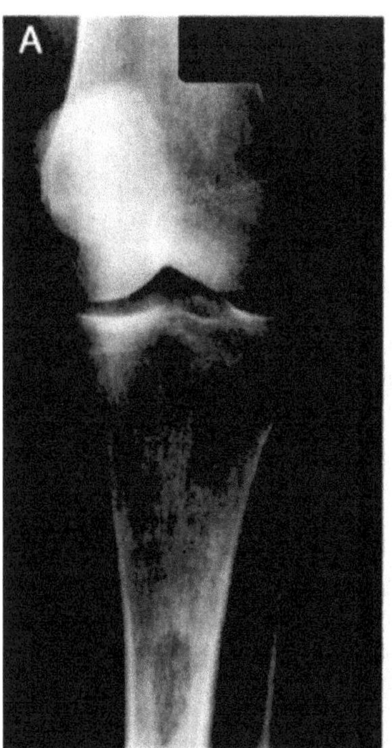
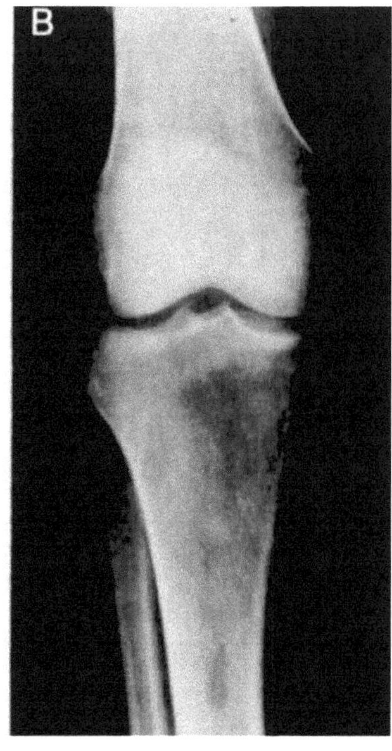

An anteroposterior view of the left knee and tibia reveals a 2.5-cm ovoid lytic lesion in the anterolateral cortex of the left tibial shaft and lucent zone in the medial half of the left patella. (B) A 2-cm ovoid lytic lesion in the anterior cortex of the proximal right tibial shaft.

20. Haematological Manifestations:

- Anemia, thrombocytopenia, hypersplenism, and leucopenia can occur.

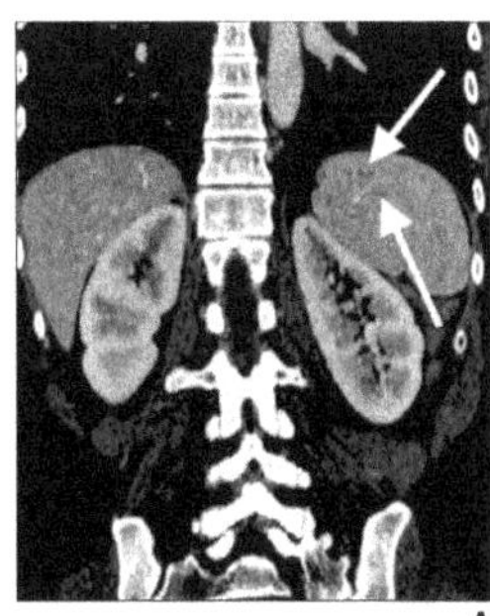
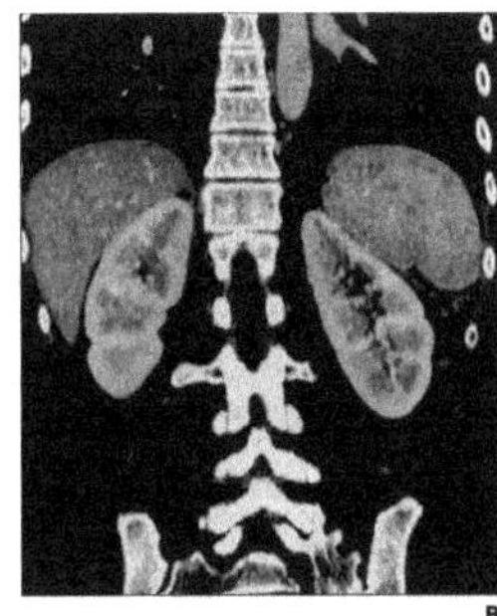
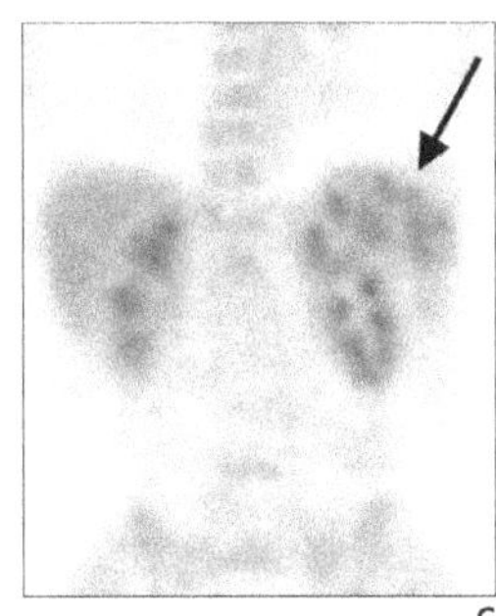

Splenic lesions with uptake from sarcoidosis in a 43-year-old woman with a history of Hodgkin's lymphoma. A–C, Images from combined PET/CT show low-density lesions (arrows, A and C) in the spleen on coronal CT image (A). Lesions show increased FDG uptake on fused PET/ CT (B) and unfused PET (C) images.

21. Gastrointestinal Manifestations:

- Rarely affects the gastrointestinal system, presenting with gastric ulcers and other symptoms.

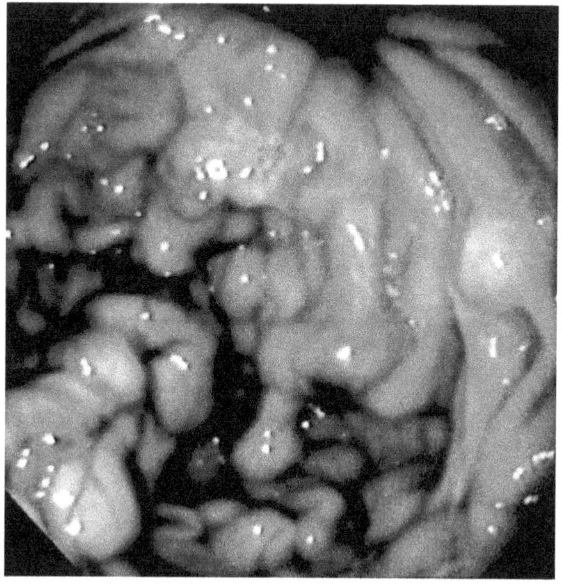

Linitis plastica syndrome

Exploring the diverse spectrum of sarcoidosis manifestations highlights its multifaceted nature and underscores the importance of comprehensive management approaches.

Criteria of Diagnosis of Sarcoidosis

For diagnosis of sarcoidosis the following criteria should be fulfilled-

1. Histological evidence of granulomatous inflammation.
2. The exclusion of the known causes of granulomatous inflammation other than sarcoidosis.
3. Evidence of at least two separate organs involved with the disease.

Examinations and Tests for Sarcoidosis

- CBC
- Chem-7 or chem-20
- ACE levels
- Chest x-ray to see if the lungs are involved or lymph nodes are enlarged
- CT scan
- Lymph node biopsy
- Skin lesion biopsy
- Bronchoscopy
- Open lung biopsy
- Liver biopsy
- Kidney biopsy
- EKG to see if the heart is involved

Sarcoidosis may also alter the results of the following tests-

- Quantitative immunoglobulins (nephelometry)
- PTH
- Serum phosphorus
- Nerve biopsy
- Mediastinoscopy with biopsy
- Lung gallium (Ga.) scan
- Immunoelectrophoresis - serum
- Calcium - urine
- Calcium - ionized
- Calcium - serum
- Liver function tests

Clinical and/or radiological patterns of sarcoidosis-

The following are all clinical and/or radiological patterns of sarcoidosis-

1. **Bilateral hilar adenopathy-** Asymptomatic patients with bilateral hilar adenopathy and no pulmonary infiltrates.
2. **Lofgren's syndrome-** A patient with a typical Lofgren's syndrome (fever, erythema nodosum, arthralgias, and bilateral hilar adenopathy).
3. **Heerfordt's syndrome-** A patient with Heerfordt's syndrome (Fever, parotid gland enlargement, facial palsy, and anterior uveitis).
4. **Panda sign-** It has been classically described as indicating Sarcoidosis.

Bilateral inflammatory involvement of the parotid and lachrymal glands results in Gallium-67 citrate uptake called as panda sign.

The presence of perihilar adenopathy adds to the lambda distribution of increased uptake in the chest, which at times has been included in the description of the panda distribution.

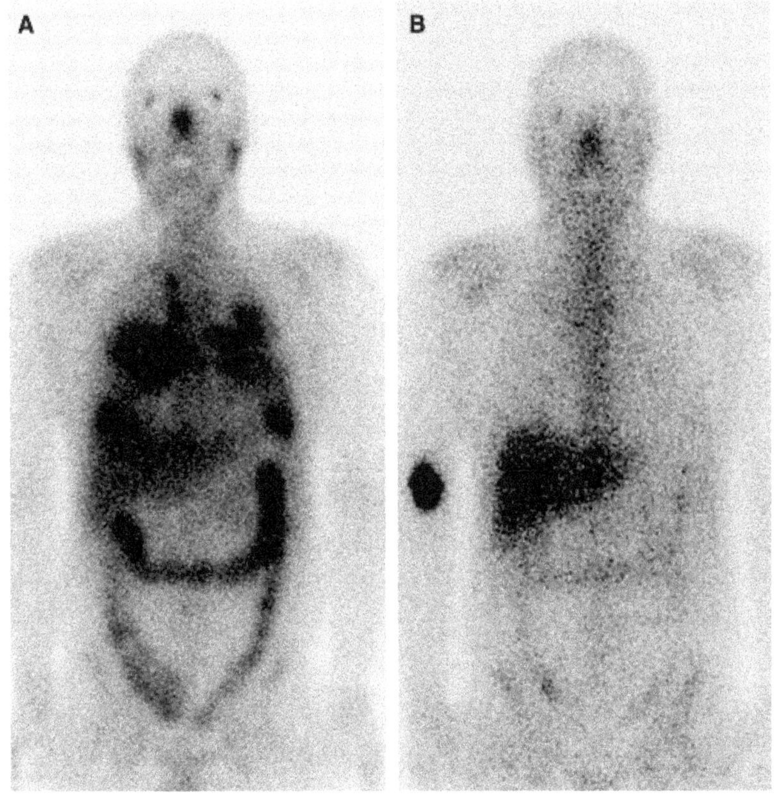

Panda sign - lachrymal and parotid uptake on a total body 67 GA scan, combined with Lambda pattern (right azygos and bilateral hilar thoracic uptake).

Enhanced Diagnosis of Sarcoidosis

Pathological Features: Sarcoidosis is characterized by distinctive granulomas, comprising compact epithelioid cells arranged radially, interspersed with multinucleate giant cells and a rim of lymphocytes.

Special stains are essential to exclude other causes of granulomatous inflammation, particularly in cases with necrotic lesions. Notably, sarcoid multinucleate giant cells often contain inclusions of calcium carbonate or calcium oxalate, which support the diagnosis.

Diagnostic Criteria: Diagnosis of sarcoidosis requires:

1. Histological evidence of granulomatous inflammation.
2. Exclusion of known causes of granulomatous inflammation apart from sarcoidosis.
3. Involvement of at least two separate organs by the disease.

Diagnostic Tests and Examinations: Various tests and examinations are crucial for diagnosis, including:

- Complete Blood Count (CBC)
- Comprehensive Metabolic Panel (Chem-7 or Chem-20)
- Serum Angiotensin Converting Enzyme (ACE) levels

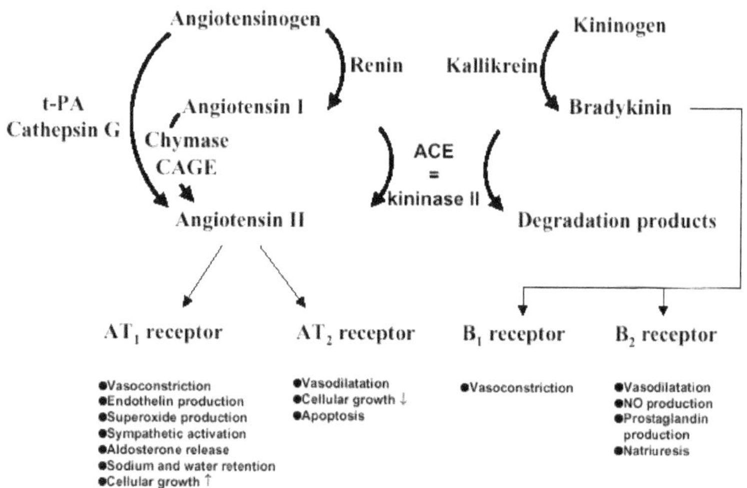

- Chest X-ray and CT scan
- Biopsies from lymph nodes, skin lesions, lungs, liver, and kidneys
- Bronchoscopy and EKG

Moreover, sarcoidosis may influence the results of additional tests, underscoring the complexity of diagnosis.

Clinical and Radiological Patterns: Distinct clinical and radiological patterns of sarcoidosis include:

1. Bilateral hilar adenopathy
2. Lofgren's syndrome
3. Heerfordt's syndrome
4. Panda sign

The Panda sign, characterized by gallium-67 uptake in the parotid and lachrymal glands, is pathognomonic for sarcoidosis when combined with a lambda distribution of increased uptake in the chest.

Additional Diagnostic Procedures:

- Pulmonary Function Test (PFT) to assess lung function

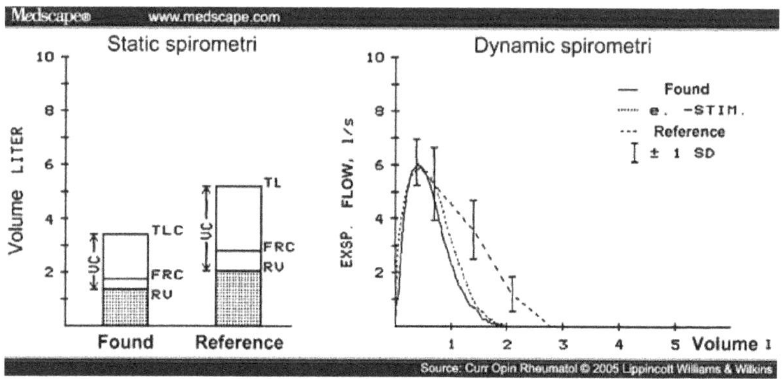

Pulmonary function test with a restrictive pattern

- Kveim-Stiltzbach test for delayed cutaneous reaction
- Tissue biopsy for histological confirmation
- Imaging techniques like bronchoalveolar lavage (BAL) and gallium scanning

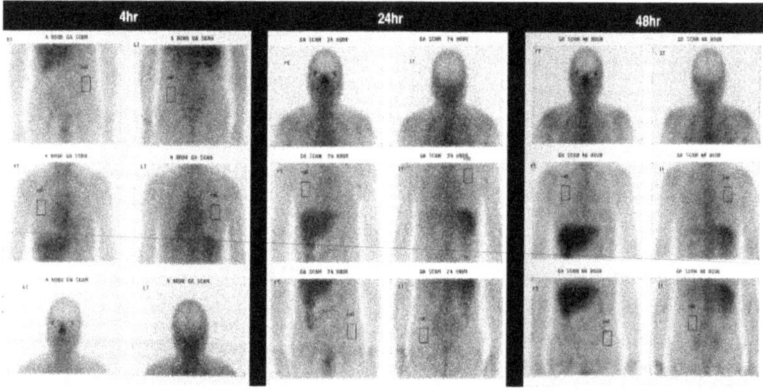

Thoracic Sarcoidosis- Gallium-67 scans in a patient who had a normal chest radiograph. Study shows increased uptake in the lung fields, higher than the background activity

Conclusion: Diagnosing sarcoidosis necessitates a comprehensive approach integrating clinical, radiological, and histological findings. Awareness of distinct patterns and appropriate utilization of diagnostic tests are pivotal for accurate diagnosis and effective management of sarcoidosis.

CHAPTER EIGHT

AN ATALAS OF SARCOIDOSIS BIOPSIES

Below here is an atlas of biopsy slides prepared from various samples taken from different organs-

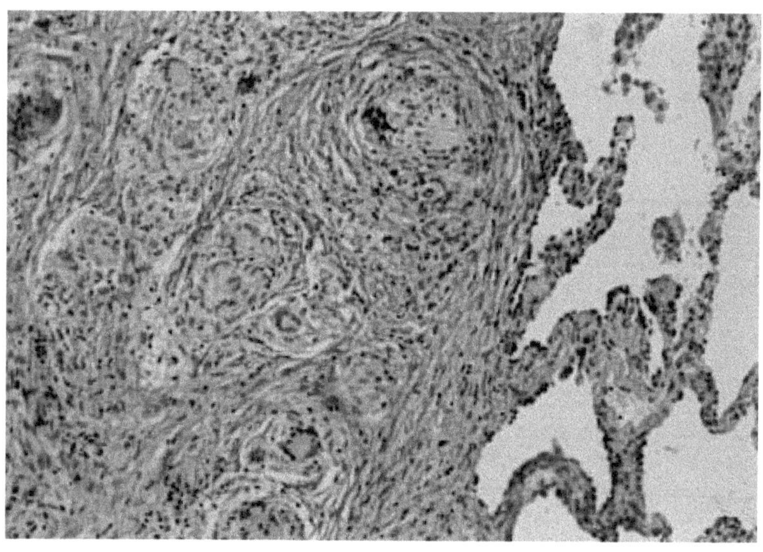

Pulmonary interstitial non-caseating granulomatous inflammation. Giant cells and histiocytes form nodular aggregates without necrosis

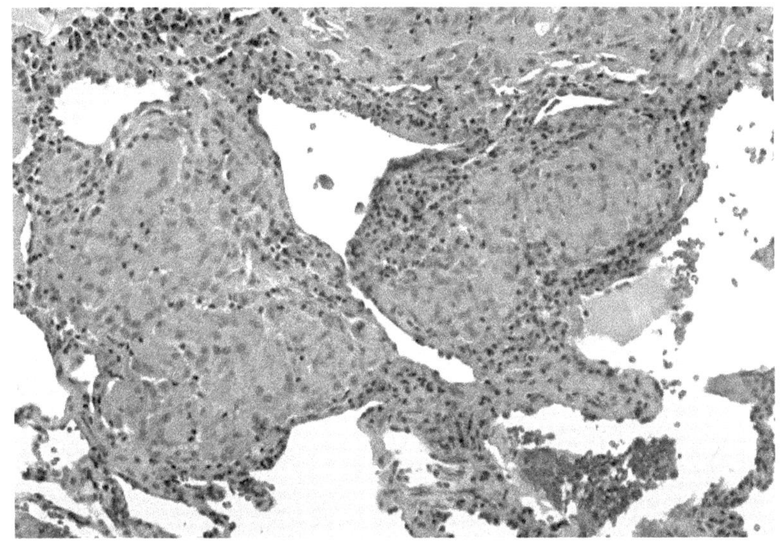

Pulmonary Interstitial granulomas

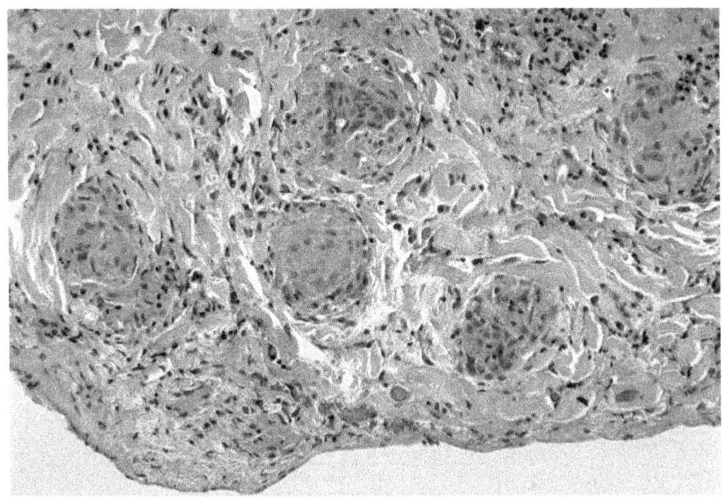

Granulomas involving visceral pleura

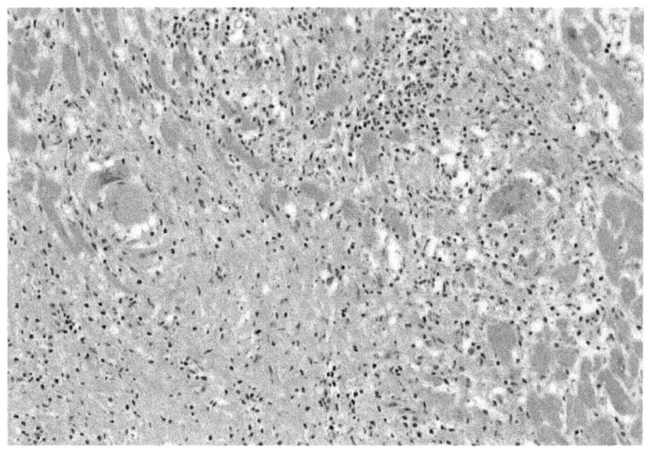

Heart- Granulomatous (giant cell) myocarditis, medium
magnification

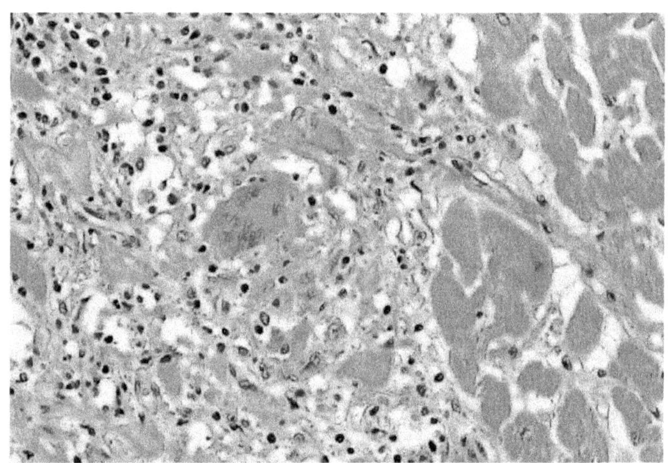

Heart- Granulomatous (giant cell) myocarditis, high
magnification

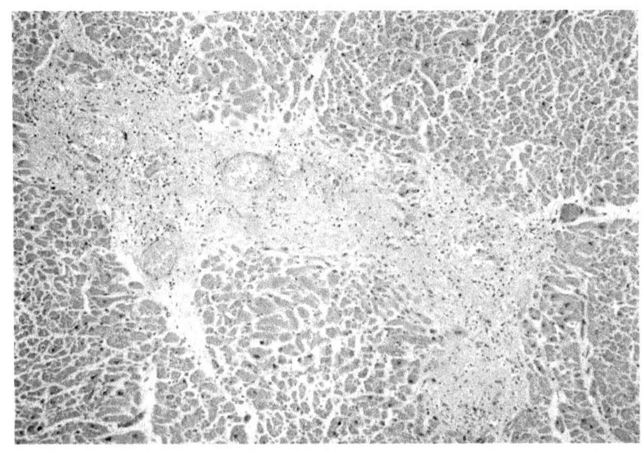

Liver - Granulomas and fibrosis involving portal triad.

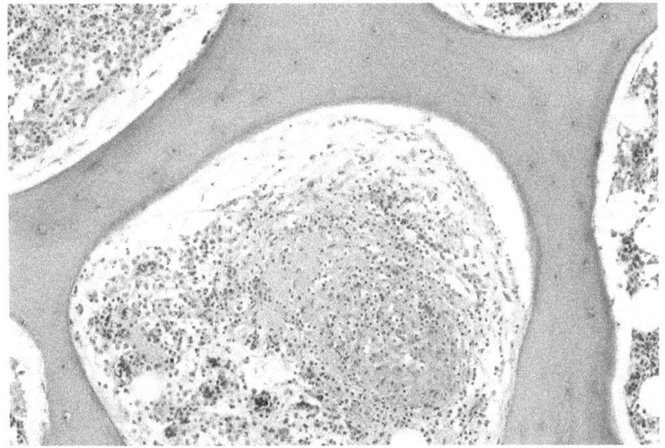

Bone marrow

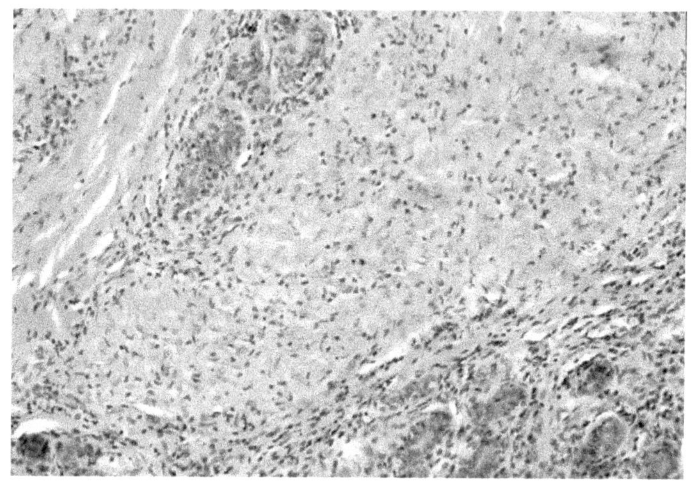

Female breast

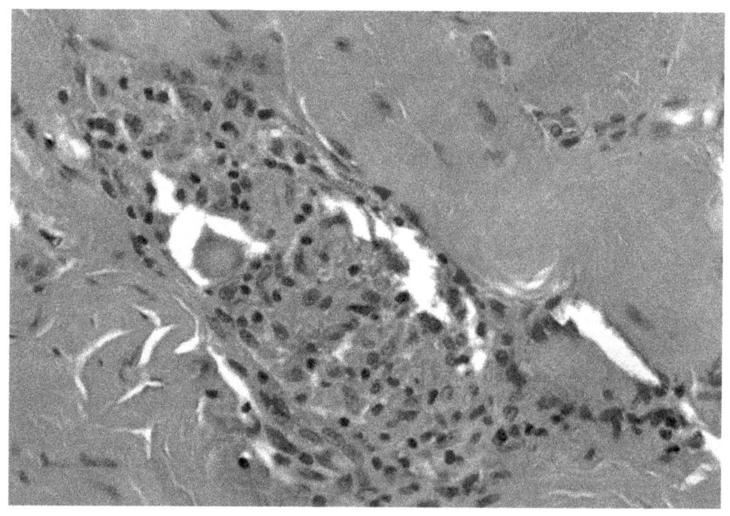

Skeletal muscle

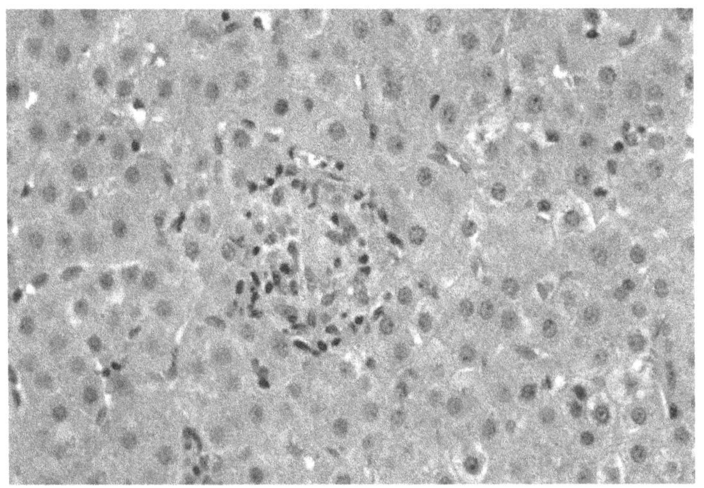

Liver – Parenchymal granuloma

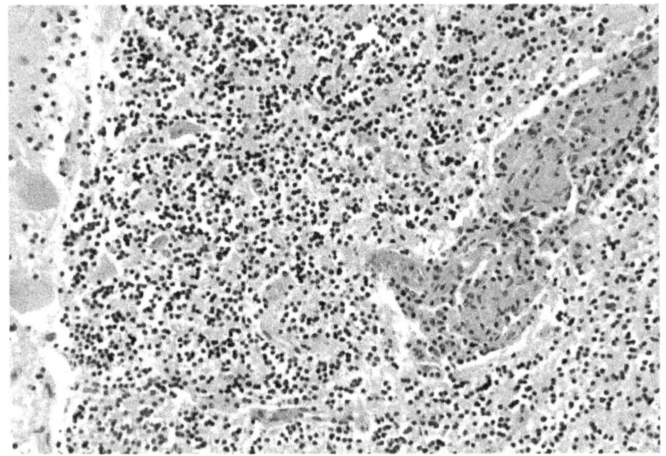

Brain, cerebellum, granulomatous angiitis

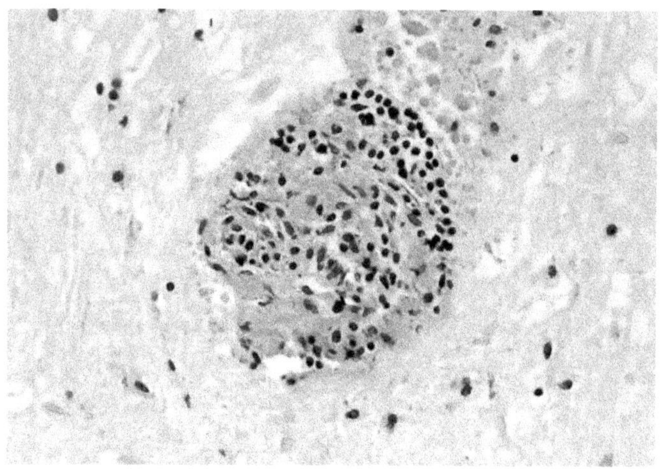

Brain, granulomatous angiitis

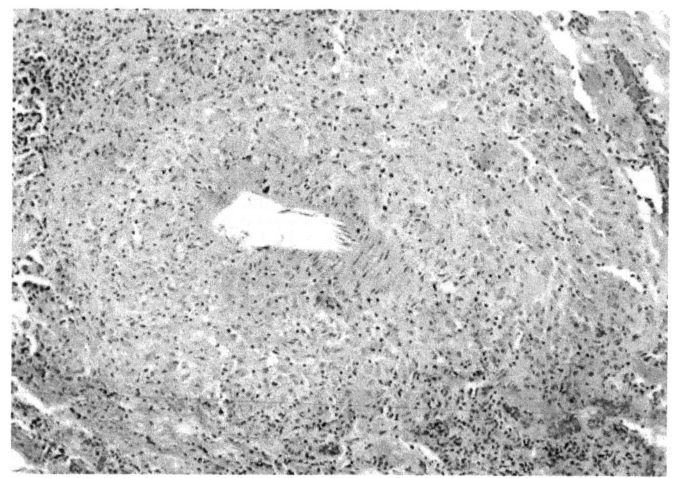

Peritoneum, granulomatous angiitis

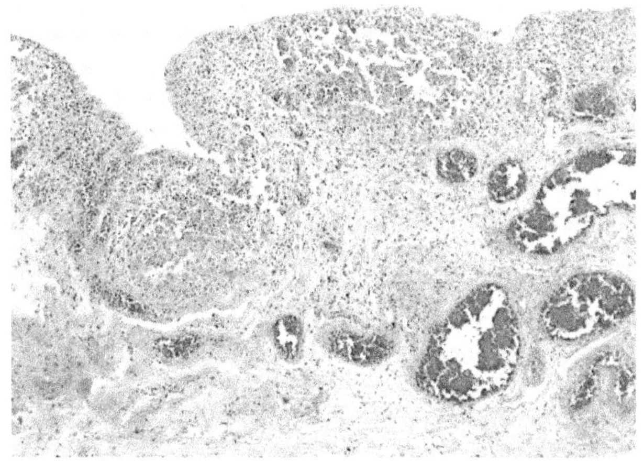

Urinary bladder

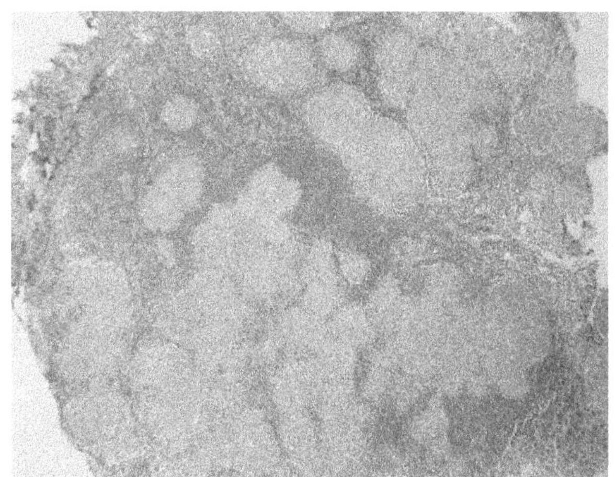

Mediastinal lymph node

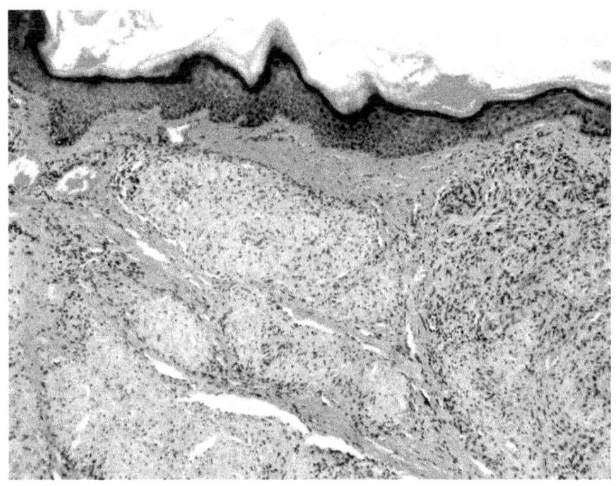

Skin Lesion in Sarcoidosis

CHAPTER NINE

PATHOLOGICAL DIFFERENTIAL DIAGNOSIS

Pathological Differential Diagnosis-

Lungs

- Tuberculosis, atypical mycobacteriosis
- Fungal: histoplasmosis, coccidioidomycosis, cryptococcosis, blastomycosis, aspergillosis
- PCP (Pneumocystis Pneumonia), mycoplasma
- Pneumoconioses: beryllium, titanium, aluminum
- Drug reactions
- Hypersensitivity pneumonitis
- Aspiration of foreign materials
- Wegener's granulomatosis
- CIP (cellular interstitial pneumonitis)- all variants e.g. UIP (usualinterstitial pneumonitis) LIP (lymphoid interstitial pneumonitis) and DIP (desquamative interstitial pneumonitis).
- NSG (necrotizing sarcoid granulomatosis)

Lymph Node

- TB, atypical mycobacteriosis
- Brucellosis
- Toxoplasmosis
- Granulocytic histiocytic necrotizing lymphadenitis (Kikuchi's disease)
- Cat scratch disease
- Sarcoid reaction in regional Lymph nodes to carcinoma
- Hodgkin's disease
- NHL (non-Hodgkin's lymphoma)
- GLUS (granulomatous lesions of unknown significance)

Skin

- TB, atypical mycobacteriosis
- Fungal infections
- Reaction to foreign bodies: beryllium, zirconium, tattooing, paraffin, etc.
- Rheumatoid nodules
- Liver
- TB, Brucellosis
- Schistosomiasis
- PBC (Primary Biliary Cirrhosis)
- Crohn's disease
- Hodgkin's and NHL
- GLUS (Granulomatous lesions of unknown significance)
- Bone Marrow
- TB, histoplasmosis, IM (Infectious Mononucleosis), CMV (Cytomegalovirus)
- Hodgkin's and NHL

- Drugs
- GLUS (Granulomatous lesions of unknown significance)
- Other organs
- TB, brucellosis
- Giant cell myocarditis

The Conditions "possible but most unlikely" with sarcoidosis-

1. No evidence of extrapulmonary disease (chronic berylliosis, other possible granulomatous lung disease).
2. No thoracic lymphadenopathy on radiographic studies (hypersensitivity pneumonitis, other granulomatous lung disease).
3. The patient with a very low likelihood of having sarcoidosis (e.g., young age).

Some important differential diagnoses of sarcoidosis-

The differential diagnosis depends largely on the clinical presentation of sarcoidosis. Granulomatous pulmonary infections, especially those caused by mycobacteria and fungi should be ruled out. Neoplastic diseases, such as lymphoma, in cases with hilar adenopathy, should be excluded.

Hypercalcemia in sarcoidosis may mimic metabolic disorders, such as primary hyperparathyroidism. Early onset sarcoidosis is often misdiagnosed as systemic-onset juvenile rheumatoid arthritis (JRA). Rarely, severe symptomatic bone marrow involvement may mimic several infectious and neoplastic disorders.

Necrotizing Sarcoid Granulomatosis

Necrotizing sarcoid granulomatosis (NSG) has an uncertain relationship to sarcoidosis. The NSG lesion represents a sarcoid granuloma with necrosis and vasculitis. Some authors consider it a variant of sarcoidosis.

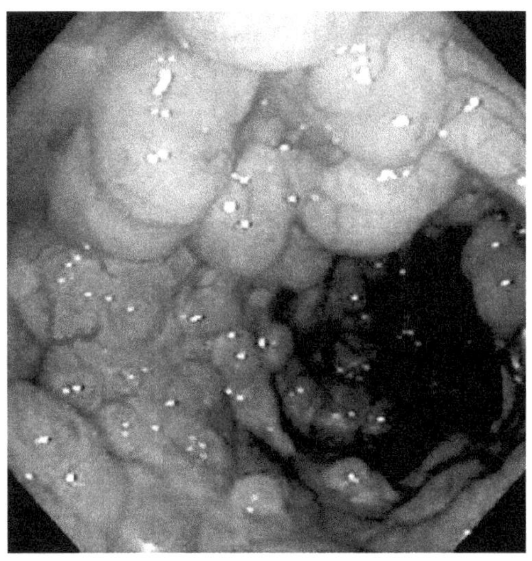

Necrotizing sarcoid granulomatosis

Erdheim–Chester Disease

It is a rare histiocytic disorder of adults characterized by an infiltrate of lipid-laden macrophages, multinucleated giant cells, an inflammatory infiltrate of lymphocytes and histiocytes in the bone marrow, and generalized sclerosis of the long bones sparing the epiphysis. Bone involvement is constant but the kidney, retroperitoneal space, skin, brain, and lungs are also affected.

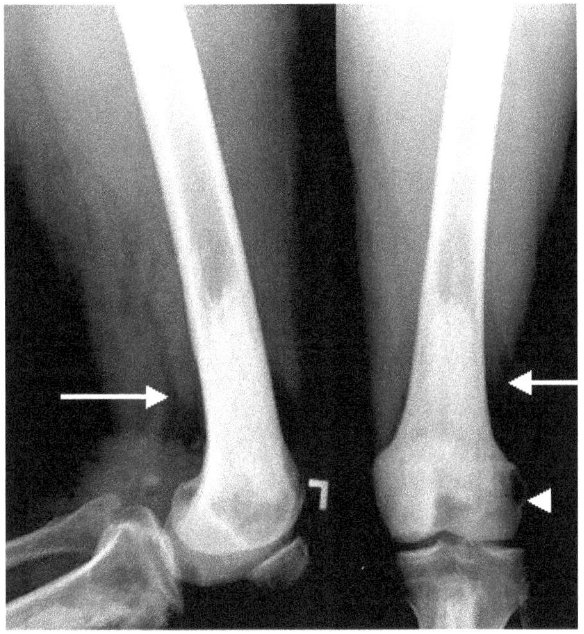

Ill defined sclerosis of the distal femur extending to the epiphysis of the medial femoral condyle (arrows) and sparing the lateral condyle (arrowhead)

Granulomatous Lesions of Unknown Significance

Granulomatous lesions of unknown significance (GLUS syndrome) are described clinically as prolonged fever with epithelioid granulomas in the liver, bone marrow, spleen, and lymph nodes. It has a benign course and a tendency for recurrence.

Blau's Syndrome

Blau's syndrome is an autosomal dominant condition with variable penetration that consists of granulomatous arthritis, iritis, and skin rash, occurring before 12 years of age.

Prognosis of Sarcoidosis

In many people, sarcoidosis is usually asymptomatic and the disease may resolve without treatment. 30 - 50% of cases resolve without treatment in about 3 years. About 20% of those with lung involvement develop lung damage.

Death from sarcoidosis is rare. The mortality rate is less than 3%. Pulmonary fibrosis leading to cardiopulmonary resuscitation failure is the most common cause of death. About 10% have a serious disability such as ocular or respiratory. Pulmonary hemorrhage from aspergilloma is an acute complication.

Common Complications of Sarcoidosis

- Diffuse interstitial pulmonary fibrosis
- Pulmonary hypertension
- Anterior uveitis
- Glaucoma and blindness (rare)
- Cardiac arrhythmias
- Cranial or peripheral nerve palsies
- Kidney stones
- Organ failure, leading to the need for a transplant

Sarcoidosis Management and Treatment

Main Goals of Treatment:

- Enhance organ function affected by sarcoidosis
- Alleviate symptoms
- Reduce the size of granulomas

Treatment Approach:

The course of treatment is tailored based on:

- Present symptoms and their severity
- Vital organ involvement (e.g., lungs, eyes, heart, brain)
- Extent of organ affection

Individualized Management:

- Treatment necessity varies; some organs may require intervention regardless of symptoms, while others may not

necessitate immediate treatment.
- Asymptomatic cases often require no treatment, with patients often experiencing spontaneous recovery over time.

Managing Sarcoidosis:

- Regular medical evaluations are crucial for monitoring the disease's progression and adjusting treatment as necessary during active phases.
- Even during periods of inactivity or absence of symptoms, annual checkups, particularly ophthalmological exams, are essential.
- Ceasing smoking is imperative as it can exacerbate the condition.
- Avoidance of lung-harming substances like dust, chemicals, and fumes is advised.
- Physical activity should be maintained within the patient's capacity, avoiding excessive strain.

Conclusion:

With appropriate management and lifestyle adjustments, many individuals with sarcoidosis can maintain a normal quality of life, engaging in social, intellectual, artistic, and physical activities.

CHAPTER ELEVEN

An Exploration of Sarcoidosis in the Context of Homeopathy

In a groundbreaking clinical study titled "Homoeopathy in Sarcoidosis with Miasmatic Concepts," unique insights emerged:

- **Sex Incidence:** Females were notably more affected than males, with a distribution of 4% for males and 7% for females.
- **Age Incidence:** Sarcoidosis was most prevalent among individuals aged 31-50, with lower incidences in prepuberty and the elderly.
- **Marital Status Incidence:** Married individuals comprised 82% of cases, while singles represented 18%.
- **Physical Built Incidence:** Moderate-built individuals showed the highest occurrence of Sarcoidosis.
- **Caste Incidence:** Hindus exhibited a higher susceptibility compared to Muslims and Sikhs.
- **Occupational Incidence:** Working individuals accounted for 46% of cases, followed by housewives (27%), students (18%), and non-working individuals (9%).
- **Socioeconomic Incidence:** Sarcoidosis prevalence was highest among the affluent (46%) and lowest among the average (20%).

- **Pathological Incidence:** Idiopathic Sarcoidosis was the most frequent (100%), followed by Sarcoidosis with pulmonary manifestations (55%), and Sarcoidosis with arthritis (37%).
- **Menstrual Incidence:** Females without menses, particularly those with amenorrhoea or postmenopausal status, exhibited maximum occurrence. Normal menstruating females had a higher incidence compared to those with scanty menses.
- **Miasmatic Incidence:** Sycosis emerged as the predominant miasm-causing Sarcoidosis (37%), followed by Psora (36%) and Pseudopsora (27%).
- **Mode of Prescription:** Treatment was based on the totality of symptoms, employing mental to physical generals and particulars, or rare and peculiar symptoms where available.
- **Gross Cure Incidence:** Homoeopathic treatment demonstrated remarkable efficacy, with a cure rate of 27%, relief of 73%, and no instances of non-cure.
- **Cure Incidence based on Socioeconomic Status:** Cure rates were highest among poor patients and lowest among the affluent.
- **Cure Incidence based on Menstrual States:** Normal menstruating females showed a 50% cure rate, while those with scanty menses or amenorrhoea/postmenopausal status experienced 100% relief.
- **Cure Incidence based on Miasms:** Sycosis exhibited the highest cure rate at 50%, with 50% relief, while Psora showed no cure but 100% relief. Pseudopsora cases saw a 33% cure rate with 67% relief.

CHAPTER TWELVE

HOMOEOPATHY: A COMPREHENSIVE OVERVIEW

Introduction to Homoeopathy:

Homoeopathy, pioneered by Dr. Christian Frederick Samuel Gottfried Hahnemann of Germany, is a system of treatment founded on well-defined laws and principles.

Key Principles:

The Law of Similars: Also known as the Law of Cure, this principle posits that a substance capable of producing symptoms in a healthy individual can cure similar symptoms in a diseased individual. For instance, a remedy derived from onion may treat symptoms resembling those of acute colds.

The Law of Single Remedy: Advocates the use of a single remedy that closely matches the symptom complex of the patient at a given time.

The Law of Minimum Dose: Emphasizes the administration of remedies in minimal doses to avoid toxic effects while stimulating the body's defense mechanisms.

Holistic Approach and Individualization:

Homoeopathy adopts a holistic approach, treating the entire individual rather than just the disease manifestation. Each patient is regarded as a unique entity, with treatment tailored to their mental, emotional, and physical symptoms.

Vital Force:

Homoeopathy acknowledges the presence of a vital force, an invisible life energy that permeates all living organisms. This force maintains harmony and vitality within the body, as described by Dr. Hahnemann.

Chronic Diseases and Miasms:

Hahnemann identified chronic diseases as those characterized by a slow and insidious onset, often caused by underlying infectious miasms. These miasms, including Psora, Sycosis, Syphilis, and Pseudo-psora, contribute to predispositions and complex pathologies.

Signs and Symptoms of Miasms:

Each miasm presents characteristic signs and symptoms, influencing the physical constitution, temperament, pains, discharges, and skin manifestations of the individual. Understanding these miasms aids in selecting appropriate remedies.

Totality, Constitution, and Miasms:

In Homoeopathy, the totality of symptoms, constitution, and underlying miasms form the basis of treatment. Identifying the fundamental cause, along with the individual's constitution, guides remedy selection for chronic disorders like Sarcoidosis.

Idiosyncrasy and Indisposition:

Idiosyncrasy refers to an individual's hypersensitivity to certain stimuli, making them more susceptible to illnesses like Sarcoidosis. Indisposition, on the other hand, denotes a slight deviation from health that often resolves spontaneously with minor adjustments.

Conclusion:

Homoeopathy offers a unique approach to healthcare, focusing on individualized treatment, adherence to natural laws, and the restoration of the body's innate healing abilities. By addressing the root cause of illness and considering the holistic well-being of the patient, it aims to promote long-term health and vitality.

Miasmatic Analysis of Signs and Symptoms associated with 'Sarcoidosis'-

Sign or Symptom	Fundamental Miasm	Secondary/ Associated Miasm
General discomfort, uneasiness, or ill feeling (malaise)	Psora	Psora- Syphilis
Fever	Psora	
Shortness of breath	Psora	Sycosis
Cough	Psora	Sycosis, Syphilis
Skin lesions	Psora	Sycosis
Skin rash	Psora	
Headache	Psora	Sycosis, Syphilis
Visual changes	Psora-Sycosis-Syphilis	
Neurological changes	Sycosis-Syphilis	Psora
Enlarged lymph glands (armpit lump)	Psora	Sycosis
Enlarged liver	Psora	Sycosis
Enlarged spleen	Psora	Sycosis
Dry mouth	Psora	
Fatigue (one of the most common symptoms in children)	Psora	Syphilis
Weight loss (one of the most common symptoms in children)	Psora-Syphilis	
Tearing, decreased	Psora	Sycosis, Syphilis
Seizures	Psora	Psora- Syphilis
Nosebleed - symptom	Psora- Syphilis	
Joint stiffness	Psora	Sycosis
Hair loss	Psora	Sycosis, Syphilis
Eye burning, itching, and discharge	Psora	Psora- Syphilis
Abnormal breath sounds (e.g. rales)	Psora- Syphilis	Sycosis

Miasmatic Analysis of Signs and Symptoms associated with 'Sarcoidosis'

CHAPTER THIRTEEN

LITERATURE RELATED WITH 'SARCOIDOSIS' FOUND IN VARIOUS HOMOEOPATHIC BOOKS

THERAPEUTICS

1- Degroote F., Physical Examination and Observation in Homoeopathy
  Materia Medica
  Tuberculinum bovinum kent
  Clinical Observations
  Enlarged and induration of glands. Sarcoidosis.
2- Indian Journal of Homoeopathic Medicine-1995- vol. 30
  Homoeopathic Approach to the Problem of Cancer
  Cancer- Sarcoidosis and Pneumoconiosis- Berrylium
3- International Foundation for Homoeopathy
  Case Conference Proceedings- 1991
  The Emerging Picture of Leprominium
  The Leprosy Nosode
  Conclusion

Leprosy resembles many skin conditions. Leprominium should be useful in many of these conditions, including leucoderma, nutritional discoloration of the skin, macular syphilides, tinea versicolor, lupus erythematosus, lupus vulgaris, neurofibromatosis, cutaneous sarcoidosis, leukemia cutis, Kaposi's sarcoma, subcutaneous phycomycosis, lymphoma, seborrheic dermatitis, erythema multiforme, alopecia areata, ringworm, psoriasis, lichen planus, pityriasis rosea, urticaria, scleroderma, lipoma, acne vulgaris, and molluscum contagiosum.

4- Murphy R. Homoeopathic Remedy Guide

Beryllium metallicum

Symptoms

Lungs

Appearance similar to tuberculosis or sarcoidosis.

5- Murphy R. Homoeopathic Remedy Guide

Beryllium metallicum

Symptomatology

Clinical Diagnosis

Generalities

Sarcoidosis.

6- Murphy R. Homoeopathic Remedy Guide

Beryllium metallicum

Symptomatology

Clinical Diagnosis

Respirator System

Pulmonary sarcoidosis.

7- Murphy R. Homoeopathic Remedy Guide

Beryllium metallicum

Symptomatology

Clinical Diagnosis

Locomotor

Sarcoidosis of the bones.

8- Liga Medicorum Homoeopathica Internationalis- 1988

Leprominium

Conclusion

Leprosy resembles many skin conditions like leucoderma, nutritional discolouration of skin, macular syphilides tinea versicolor, Lupus erythematous, lupus vulgaris, neurofibromatosis, cutaneous sarcoidosis, leukemia cutis, kaposis sarcoma, subcutaneous phycomycosis, lymphoma, seborrhoic dermatitis, erythema multiform, alopecia areata ringworm of the skin, psoriasis, lichen planus, pityriasis rosea, urticaria, scleroderma, lipoma, acne vulgaris, molluscum contagiosum, etc. It should be useful in many of these conditions.

9- Master F. J. Tubercular Miasm Tuberculins

The Secondary Symptoms of Tuberculosis

Heart

Boeck's Sarcoidosis.

10- Morrison R. Seminar Burgh Haamstede Sept 1987

Nux vomica

Case 1

Then I had another two more cases that came in, absolutely perfect cases, my first three cases. The first was Crohn's disease, the second was scleroderma - which was a Kali carbonicum, and the third was sarcoidosis - which was a Pulsatilla case. Absolutely perfect clear cases: essence, totality, keynotes - everything. Then I had to wait one year before I saw another such case! So you see that homeopathy seduces us and makes us think: "Oh, how easy, how wonderful" and then we get trapped and it makes us work very hard.

11- Morrison R. Seminar Burgh Haamstede Sept 1987

Remarks, Questions

Sstudying Homoeopathy

Usually long before you think you are ready you should start. Because if you don't start, you cannot learn. You have to make sure to start the practice with simple cases. Don't do what I did and start with Crohn's disease and sarcoidosis. But start with headaches, arthritis, and simple cases first.

12- Murphy R. Homoeopathic Remedy Guide

Beryllium metallicum

Clinical

Allergic conditions. Cancerous conditions. Chronic fatigue syndrome. Kidney stones. Sarcoidosis. Tubercular conditions.

13- Murphy R. Homoeopathic Remedy Guide

Beryllium metallicum

Limbs

Rheumatism. Pain in the arms as if bruised. Buttocks cold. Clubbed fingers. Blue discoloration of the hands. Sarcoidosis of the bones. Deposits around the inter-phalangeal joints.

14- Murphy R. Homoeopathic Remedy Guide

Beryllium metallicum

Lungs

Respiration is painful, aggravated by movement. Cough deep, dry, painful, aggravated by bending backward. Aggravated by smoke, improved in a very warm room. Sputum streaked with blood. Cyanosis, cough accelerating the respiratory rhythm. Spasmodic cough with pain behind the sternum. Appearance is similar to tuberculosis or sarcoidosis. Tracheitis and bronchitis. Capillary bronchitis. Dilation of the bronchi. Pulmonary sarcoidosis. Pneumoconiosis. Pulmonary tuberculosis, early stage. Emphysema.

15- Scholten J. – Homoeopathy And The Elements

Carbon Series: Lithium to Neon

Beryllium metallicum

Beryllium is known to cause a disease picture that is almost identical to sarcoidosis (also called Besnier-Boeck disease). Julian (1979, 1981) has described a proving of Beryllium.

16- Scholten J. – Homoeopathy and The Elements

Carbon Series: Lithium to Neon

Beryllium metallicum

Picture of Beryllium Metallicum

Complaints

Lung affection: sarcoidosis, cancer.

17- Scholten J. – Homoeopathy And The Elements

Ferrum Sereis: Kali ti Krypton

Manganum sulphuricum

Case by Rienk Stuut

She eats a lot. An X-ray of her lungs showed she had sarcoidosis.

18- Scholten J. – Homoeopathy And The Elements

Ferrum Sereis: Kali ti Krypton

Manganum sulphuricum

Case by Rienk Stuut

Reaction

The pains in her knee had disappeared by the next day. The dizziness also went away quite soon and the tiredness disappeared after an initial aggravation. For the first time in her life, she feels completely fit and well. The sarcoidosis also disappeared. One year after she got the remedy she still feels fine and she looks radiant.

19- Schroyens F.- Synthesis (Original English Version)- 9th Ed.

Natrium arsenicosum

Chest

CHEST - SARCOIDOSIS pulmonalis

20- Van Woensel E., Radar Keynotes Version 4

Characteristics and Peculiarities

A Compiled Materia Medica

Beryllium metallicum

Respiratory Tract

Tuberculosis. Sarcoidosis.

21- Vermeulen F.- Prisma- Materia Medica

Calcarea carbonica

Signs

HYPERCALCEMIA Prolonged administration of calcium carbonate may result in hypercalcemia, producing confused behavior, anorexia, abdominal pain, and weak muscles, possibly leading to the development of kidney stones and impaired kidney function. When bred after a week on diets supplemented with high amounts of calcium, female mice produced young which were lower in weight and number. Mortality was increased. The highest level of supplemented calcium carbonate caused heart enlargement. In humans, five hundred milligrams per kilogram of body weight was fed to ulcer victims for three weeks - 145 times the normal ingested amount. Apart from hypercalcemia, some patients suffered from nausea, weakness, and dizziness. A rare syndrome occurring in very young children, named idiopathic hypercalcemia, results in osteosclerosis, renal insufficiency, and sometimes hypertension; may also be associated with supravalvular aortic stenosis, mental retardation, and elfin facies. The latter is characterized by a short, upturned nose, wide mouth, widely spaced eyes, and full cheeks. Primary causes of hypercalcemia are [1] parathyroid hormone excess; [2] malignancy with bone metastases; [3] hyperthyroidism; [4] vitamin D intoxication; vitamin A intoxication; [5] excessive gastrointestinal calcium absorption or intake; [6] sarcoidosis; [7] myxedema, Addison's disease, postoperative Cushing's disease; [8] lithium intoxication; [9] aluminium-induced osteomalacie; [10] immobilization, e.g. in young, growing individuals, in elderly patients with osteoporosis, and in paraplegics or quadriplegics. Symptoms of mild hypercalcemia include constipation, anorexia, nausea and vomiting with abdominal pain and ileus. In more severe cases, there is emotional lability, confusion, delirium, psychosis, stupor, and coma. Neuromuscular involvement may cause prominent skeletal muscle weakness. Hypercalciuria with nephrolithiasis or urolithiasis is common. Peptic ulcers and pancreatitis may be associated with hyperparathyroidism. 7

22- Vermeulen F.

Prisma

Materia Medica

Colchicum autumnale

Signs

COLCHICINE The major alkaloid of Colchicum autumnale is colchicine. The colchicine content is highest in the seeds [up to 1,3%], followed by the corm, while the leaves and flowers have the lowest content. Pure colchicine consists of pale yellow scales or powder, darkening on exposure to light. Its biological activities include antimitotic, anti-inflammatory, and antifibrogenic actions. It also acts on liver functions: it modifies membrane fluidity, and increases membrane enzymes activities and glycogen levels. Colchicine is used to treat acute gout, familial mediterranean fever, and, less frequently, leukemia, and Behçet's syndrome. More recently, the use of colchicine has expanded to include such indications as primary biliary cirrhosis, alcohol-induced cirrhosis, sarcoidosis, and scleroderma. Because it inhibits collagen transport to the extracellular space, it is employed in the prevention or treatment of amyloidosis and scleroderma. Colchicine has been shown to be more toxic in the elderly, especially those with liver or kidney dysfunction. Patients are advised to consume a large amount of fluids while taking colchicine. Although research is inconsistent, colchicine is believed to prevent vitamins A and B12 absorption. It has also been associated with impaired absorption of beta-carotene, fat, lactose, potassium, and sodium. Acidifying agents inhibit the action of colchicine, while alkalinizing agents potentiate it. Highly toxic, death has resulted from single oral doses of 3 to 13 mg colchicine, although the estimated lethal dose is 20-65 mg. In laboratory animals, this alkaloid has caused both birth defects and damage to the reproductive system.

23- Vermeulen F.

Synoptic Materia Medica 2

Beryllium metallicum

Leading Symptoms

P Sarcoidosis [Besnier-Boeck-Schaumann disease].

24- Vithoulkas G. Materia Medica Viva

Arsenicum bromatum

The Essential Features

This is a remedy that should be thought of in cases of cancerous affections or affections involving the glands with swelling and induration. Hodgkin's disease, sarcoidosis, tuberculosis and infectious mononucleosis may be classed under its pathology. It will suit cases of diabetis mellitus and insipidus, accompanied by a dramatic loss of weight and excessive thirst, and cases presenting an excessive amount of sugar in the urine in diabetis mellitus. It will also suit cases of nephritis.

25- Vithoulkas G. Materia Medica Viva

Arsenicum iodatum

Generalities

Inflammation of glands, bones and serous membranes. Hodgkin's disease. Sarcoidosis. Mucus secretions increased, copious catarrhal discharges, thick and yellow resembling yellow honey, or yellow-green.

26- Yasgur J. Homoeopathic Dictionary

Dictionary

Boeck's Sarcoid

(sarcoidosis, Besnier-Boeck-Schaumann syndrome) a connective tissue tumor, usually highly malignant, and of unknown origin, which involves the lungs, lymph nodes, skin, liver, spleen, eyes, bones of the fingers and toes, and parotid glands. These tissues gradually become fibrous (harden). Named after P.M. Boeck (1845-1917), a Norwegian dermatologist. 'Sarcoid' means 'resembling flesh'.

CHAPTER FOURTEEN

REPERTORY OF SARCOIDOSIS

Repertory of Sarcoidosis

CHEST - SARCOIDOSIS pulmonalis

ars-br. Ars-i. Beryl. lyc. Mang-s. nat-ar. parathyr. pin-s. puls. Tub-m. tub. v-a-b.

CHEST - SARCOIDOSIS, pulmonary

beryl. nat-ar.

SKIN - SARCOIDOSIS

beryl.

GENERALITIES - BESNIER-BOECK, morbus, Sarcoidosis

aq-mar. aran-ix. asar. beryl. hip-ac. hist. kres. lepr. lyc. mand. nat-ar. parathyr. pin-s. puls. thiop. tub-m. tub. v-a-b.

EYE - INFLAMMATION - Iris

acon. Apis Arg-n. ARN. Ars-i. ars-s-f. Ars. Asaf. aur-ar. aur-i. aur-s. Aur. Bell. BRY. calc-hi. calc. Cedr. Chin. chinin-m. Cinnb. Clem. Colch. Coloc. Com. con. crot-h. Crot-t. dub. Dulc. Euphr. ferr-p. gels. grin. ham. Hep. iod. Kali-bi. Kali-i. kalm. lepr. MERC-C. merc-i-f. merc-pn. Merc. mez. morg-p. Nat-m. nat-sal. Nit-ac. nux-v. petr. phyt. plb. Puls. RHUS-T. sabal sal-ac. Seneg. Sil. spig. Staph. sul-i. Sulph. Syph. tell. Ter. thuj. toxo-g. vac. zinc.

EYE - INFLAMMATION - Iris - adhesions, with

Calc. Clem. graph. Merc-c. Nit-ac. sil. spig. staph. Sulph. Ter.

FACE - DISCOLORATION - bluish

absin. acon. agar-ph. Agar. Ail. alum-p. alum-sil. am-c. aml-ns. androc. ang. ant-c. ant-t. Apis Arg-n. Ars-i. ars-s-f. ARS. ASAF. asar. asim. aur-ar. Aur. bad. BAPT. BELL. borx. both. brom. BRY. bufo Cact. cadm-met. calc-p. calc. CAMPH. CANN-I. Canth. Carb-an. CARB-V. Carbn-s. carl. Caust. Cedr. Cench. Cham. chinin-ar. chlf. Chlol. Chlor. Cic. cimic. Cina cinnb. Cocc. colch. CON. cor-r. croc. crot-h. crot-t. Cupr-act. CUPR. cypra-eg. cyt-l. DIG. Dros. Dulc. ferr. frag. gels. Glon. helo-s. Hep. hydr-ac. HYOS. ign. indg. iod. IP. jal. Kali-c. kali-cy. Kali-i. kali-m. kali-p. kali-sil. Kreos. LACH. lachn. Laur. loxo-lae. Lyc. mag-p. meph. merc-c. merc-cy. merc. mez. mill. MORPH. mosch. nat-ar. Nat-m. nat-p. nitro-o. Nux-v. oena. OP. ox-ac. petr. phenac. phos. Phyt. plb. prun. psor. Puls. rhus-t. russ. Samb. sang. sars. sec. sil. spig. Spong. Staph. Stram. Stry. succ-ac. sul-ac. Sulph. Tab. Tarent. tub. VERAT-V. VERAT. vesp. Vip. visc. zinc-p. zinc.

FACE - DISCOLORATION - cyanotic

anan. androc. ANT-T. ARS. atra-r. Aur. borx. both. Cact. carb-v. Cupr. hydr-ac. ix. lat-m. laur. lyss. merc-cy. NAT-M. ox-ac. physala-p. psor. russ. spig. vesp.

EXTERNAL THROAT - SWELLING - Cervical Glands

acon-l. acon. aesc. aeth. Agar. agath-a. aids. alum-sil. Alum. Alumn. Am-c. Am-m. ambr. ant-c. ant-t. Apis aq-mar. arg-met. arn. ars-br. Ars. ARUM-T. Asaf. asar. astac. aur. bac. bamb-a. BAR-C. bar-i. BAR-M. bar-s. BELL. borx. bov. brom. Bry. calad. calc-chln. calc-f. calc-i. calc-p. calc-s. calc-sil. CALC. camph. canth. Carb-an. Carb-v. carbn-s. caust. Cham. Chel. Chin. chir-fl. chord-umb. Cic. cinnb. CIST. clem. cocc. coli. Con. cupr. Dig. diph. dros. Dulc. ferr-i. ferr. glon. GRAPH. hecla Hell. helodr-cal. Hep. hydrog. ign. Iod. irid-met. kali-bi. KALI-C. Kali-chl. Kali-i. kali-m. kali-sil. ketogl-ac. kiss. kola kreos. Lach. Lap-a. lap-la. led. Lith-c. luna LYC. Mag-m. mag-p. marb-w. Merc-c. merc-cy. Merc-d. Merc-i-f. Merc-i-r. MERC. mez. moni. Morb. mur-ac. nabal. Nat-c. Nat-m. Nat-s. Nit-ac. Nux-v. ozone Petr. Ph-ac. Phos. Phyt. plb. polys. pot-e. Psor. Puls. ran-s. rhus-r. RHUS-T. rhus-v. ruta sabad. sal-fr. sal-mar. sars. scarl. sel.

Sep. SIL. Spig. Spong. stann. STAPH. staphycoc. stict. Still. streptoc. suis-em. sul-ac. sul-i. SULPH. syc. syph. tarent. tep. Thuj. Toxo-g. Tub. urol-h. v-a-b. ven-m. verat. vesp. viol-t. wies. zinc.

EXTERNAL THROAT - SWELLING - Cervical Glands - suppurative

CALC. Cist. Hep. Lith-c. MERC. Nit-ac. SIL. Sulph. Tub. v-a-b.

ABDOMEN - ENLARGED - Liver

aconin. aesc. agar. aloe anders. anis. ant-t. ars-i. Ars. aur-ar. aur-i. Aur-m. aur-s. aur. bar-m. boerh-d. brass-n-o. Bry. bufo caesal-b. Calc-ar. calc-sil. Calc. Carb-v. carc. card-m. Chel. CHIN. chinin-ar. Chion. Cocc. coloc. Con. Dig. eberth. eup-per. ferr-ar. ferr-i. ferr-p. Ferr. Fl-ac. glyc. graph. Hep. Hippoz. hydr. Iod. kali-br. Kali-c. kali-s. lac-e. lach. lact. lat-m. Laur. loxo-lae. loxo-recl. luf-b. LYC. mag-c. MAG-M. mang-act. Merc-d. merc-i-r. Merc. mur-ac. Nat-m. NAT-S. Nit-ac. Nux-m. NUX-V. Phos. pin-s. plb. Podo. pop-cand. ptel. sec. sel. senn. sep. sil. stel. sul-i. Sulph. symph. tab. tarax. thuj. toxo-g. Tub. urt-u. vip. zinc-p. Zinc.

ABDOMEN - ENLARGED - Spleen

aconin. agar. agn. anders. Anthraci. Aran. ars-br. Ars-i. ars-s-f. Ars. Aur-m. bell-p. brass-n-o. brom. calc-ar. calc-i. Calc. Caps. carb-v. card-m. CEAN. cedr. CHIN. chinin-ar. Chinin-s. chion. cimx. Cit-v. Cocc. Con. dros. ferr-act. ferr-ar. ferr-i. Ferr-m. ferr-p. Ferr. grin. Helia. Hippoz. hydr. Ign. IOD. kali-br. kali-m. Lach. laur. leucas-a. loxo-lae. loxo-recl. luf-b. mag-m. malar. merc-i-r. Nat-m. Nit-ac. nux-m. Nux-v. Op. Ph-ac. Phos. plb-i. plb. polyg-h. Polym. QUERC. Ran-s. rhus-t. rub-t. ruta saroth. squil. staphycoc. succ. Sul-ac. sul-i. Sulph. tab. tinas. toxo-g. tub. Urt-u. xanrhi.

ABDOMEN - SWELLING - Inguinal region - Glands, of

alum. am-c. anan. ant-c. Apis ars. Asaf. aur-m. aur-s. Aur. bac. BAD. bapt. Bar-c. Bar-m. Bell. brom. Bufo calc-ar. Calc-p. CALC. Carb-an. carb-v. carc. caust. Chel. Chin. cinnb. CLEM. cocc. Con. cop. crot-h. Cupr. DULC. elaps eupi. Ferr. gels. Graph. HEP. Hippoz. Iod. Kali-c. Kali-i. lac-c. LACH. lat-m. lyc. Lyss. med. MERC-C. Merc-i-f. Merc-i-r. MERC. nat-ar. Nat-c. nat-m. NIT-AC. nux-v. oci. ozone pall. ph-ac. phos. Phyt. pin-s. Puls. Rhus-t. sal-al. sep. Sil. sin-

n. spong. stann. Staph. stram. sul-i. SULPH. sumb. Syph. tarent-c. tarent. tep. Thuj. Tub. xero. zinc.

CHEST - SWELLING

ars. bell. bry. cadm-s. calc. cann-s. Dulc. iod. kali-bi. kali-chl. kali-m. kali-n. merc. mez. nat-c. pot-e. rhus-t. ribo. sep. Sil. Sulph.

EXTREMITIES - INFLAMMATION - Bones

Asaf. Aur. Calc. FL-AC. mang. MERC. Mez. PH-AC. Rhus-t. SIL.

EXTREMITIES - INFLAMMATION - Fingers - Bones

Staph.

FEVER - FEVER, heat in general

abrom-a. acet-ac. ACON. aesc. aeth. agar. agn. agrosti-vg. alet. all-s. alst. alum. am-act. am-c. am-m. Ambr. anac. Ang. ant-c. ANT-T. anthraci. APIS aran. arg-met. Arist-cl. ARN. ars-h. ARS. arum-i. Arum-t. asaf. asim. astac. aur-m. aur-s. aur. Bapt. Bar-c. bar-ox-suc. basil. bell-p. BELL. ben. benz-ac. benzo. berb. bid-p. bit-ar. bol-la. both. brom. BRY. CACT. cadm-s. cain. calad. Calc. calen. calo. camph. Canch. Canth. Caps. carb-an. carb-v. Carbn-s. card-b. card-m. casc. caul. caust. cedr. cent. Cham. Chel. chim. Chin. CHININ-S. chir-fl. cic. cimic. cimx. Cina cinch. cloth. coca Cocc. Coff. Colch. colchin. coloc. colum-p. CON. convo-s. conyz-sm. cop. corn-a. corn-f. croc. crot-h. cupr. Cur. Cycl. cymbop-ci. daph. Dig. diph-t-tpt. diph. dor. dros. Dulc. eberth. echi. Elaps elat. epil. ery-m. eucal. eup-a. Eup-per. eup-pur. euph. euphr. eys. ferr-ar. FERR-P. Ferr. fic-m. Fl-ac. galv. gard-t. GELS. gent-l. Graph. guaj. guiz-sc. gymno. hedy. Hell. Hep. Hyos. hyosin. Ign. Iod. IP. iris-t. ix. kali-bi. kali-c. kali-chl. KALI-I. kali-s. Kreos. Lac-c. lacer. Lach. lachn. lat-m. Laur. Led. leptos-ih. lim. lob. loxo-lae. loxo-recl. LYC. lyss. Mag-c. mag-m. mag-s. malar. mang. markh-l. med. meny. Merc-c. Merc-cy. Merc. Merl. MEZ. micr. mik-c. mill. mom-ch. mosch. Mur-ac. muru. nat-c. NAT-M. nat-p. nat-s. nat-sal. Nit-ac. Nux-m. NUX-V. oci-g. oci-sa. ol-j. olib-sac. Op. oper. oxyt. Parathyr. parth. pert-vc. pert. petr-ra. petr. Ph-ac. phenac. PHOS. physala-p. pic-ac. pimp. pisc. plb. plect. plumbg. Podo. positr. prim-v. prin. Psor. ptel. PULS. pyre-p. pyrog. queb. ran-a. raph. rhod. RHUS-T. Rhus-v. ruta sabad. Sabin. sal-n. sal-p. salol. Samb. Sang. sapin. saroth. sarr. sars. scarl. SEC. senecma. seneg. Sep. ser-a-c. SIL. spig. SPONG. SQUIL. Stann. Staph. STRAM. Sul-ac. Sulph. Sumb. TARAX. Tarent. ter. teucr. thuj. toxo-g. triclis-g. trios. tritic-vg. tub-a. tub-m. urt-u. Valer. vario. Verat-v. VERAT. vern-am. Viol-t. wye. yohim. zinc.

SKIN - DISCOLORATION - bluish

acon. Aeth. ail. am-c. ang. Ant-t. Apis Arg-n. arn. Ars. aur-ar. aur. Bapt. Bell. bism. both. Brom. bry. bufo cadm-s. calc-sil. calc. Camph. Carb-an. CARB-V. Carbn-s. chin. chinin-ar. coca cocc. con. cop. CROT-C. Crot-h. Cupr. cur. DIG. elaps Ferr-p. gels. glon. Hydr-ac. kali-bi. Kali-br. kreos. lac-e. lac-h. LACH. lat-m. Laur. led. mang. Merc-c. merc-cy. merc. mur-ac. naja nat-m. Nux-m. NUX-V. OP. Ox-ac. oxyurn-sc. petr. ph-ac. phos. Phyt. plb. puls. rhus-t. ruta samb. Sec. sil. spong. Stram. sulph. syph. tarent-c. Tarent. thuj. thymol. VERAT-V. VERAT. vip.

SKIN - ERUPTIONS - bluish - dark

Ail. arg-n. Crot-h. Lach. Ran-b. sars. Sulph.

SKIN - ERUPTIONS - tubercles

agar. alum. am-c. Am-m. anac. ang. Ant-c. apis aran. Ars. aur. Bar-c. bar-m. bar-s. Bell. Bry. calc-p. calc-s. CALC. Carb-an. Carb-v. carbn-s. CAUST. Cic. cocc. Con. crot-h. Dulc. Fl-ac. Graph. hell. Hep. hydrc. kali-ar. Kali-bi. Kali-br. kali-c. Kali-i. kali-n. kali-s. LACH. LED. Lyc. mag-c. mag-m. mag-s. mang. merc-c. Merc. Mez. Mur-ac. nat-ar. Nat-c. Nat-m. Nit-ac. nux-v. Olnd. Petr. ph-ac. Phos. Rhus-t. sec. sel. sep. Sil. stann. Staph. sul-ac. Sulph. syph. tarax. Thuj. tub. valer. verat. Zinc.

SKIN - INDURATIONS, nodules, etc.

aeth. Agar. ail. alum. alumn. am-c. am-m. anac. ANT-C. Ant-t. antho. Apis arg-met. arg-n. Ars-i. ars-s-f. ars. aur. Bar-c. bell. berb. borx. bov. brom. Bry. bufo calc-sil. CALC. cann-s. canth. caps. Carb-an. carb-v. carbn-s. Caul. caust. Chel. chin. chlol. cic. cinnb. Clem. cocc. CON. crot-h. crot-t. dig. dros. Dulc. euph. Graph. guaj. hell. Hep. hydr. ign. Iod. ip. iris Kali-bi. kali-br. Kali-c. kali-i. kali-n. kali-s. kali-sil. kreos. lach. Led. loxo-recl. LYC. mag-c. mag-m. maland. Mang. merc-i-f. merc-i-r. Merc. mez. Mur-ac. nat-c. Nat-m. nat-s. nit-ac. nux-v. olnd. op. par. petr. ph-ac. PHOS. phyt. psor. PULS.

Ran-b. RHOD. RHUS-T. Ruta sabin. sars. Sec. sel. SEP. SIL. spig. spong. squil. stann. Staph. stram. sul-ac. SULPH. tarax. ther. Thuj. tritic-vg. tub. urt-u. valer. verat. verb. viol-t. zinc-s. zinc.

SKIN - LUPUS

abr. agar. alum-sil. alum. alumn. ant-c. apis arg-n. ars-i. ARS. aur-ar. aur-i. aur-m. Bar-c. bell. calc-i. calc-s. calc-sil. calc. calo. Carb-ac. Carb-v. Caust. chr-o. cic. Cist. cund. ferr-pic. form-ac. form. germ-met. graph. guar. guare. hep. Hydr. Hydrc. irid-met. kali-ar. Kali-bi. kali-c. Kali-chl. Kali-i. Kali-s. kali-sil. Kreos. lach. LYC. m-arct. merc-i-r. merc. nat-m. NIT-AC. nux-v. ol-j. Phyt. Psor. puls. ran-b. rhus-t. sabin. sep. Sil. sol spong. staph. sulph. thiosin. THUJ. titan. tub. urea x-ray

SKIN - NETWORK of blood vessels

ant-t. Ars. bell. berb. Calc. carb-an. Carb-v. Caust. clem. Crot-h. ferr-p. graph. hydr. kreos. lach. lyc. merc. nat-m. nit-ac. nux-v. ox-ac. petr. Phos. plat. puls. rhus-t. sabad. sec. Sep. sil. staph. sul-ac. sulph. thuj.

GENERALS - ABSCESSES - Glands

anthraci. ars. Aur-m-n. Aur. bad. Bar-c. bar-m. Bell. brom. calc-f. Calc-hp. calc-i. calc-p. CALC-S. CALC. canth. carb-an. carb-v. cinnb. cist. clem. coloc. crot-h. Dulc. echi. fl-ac. Form. Guaj. guare. HEP. hyos. ign. jug-r. KALI-I. kreos. Lach. lap-a. Lyc. MERC. moni. myris. Nit-ac. petr. Phos. Phyt. Pyrog. Rhus-t. Sars. sec. Sep. sil-mar. SIL. spig. squil. Stram. sul-ac. SULPH. Syph. teucr-s. toxo-g. Tub. v-a-b. zinc.

GENERALS - EMACIATION

ABROT. acal. Acet-ac. adren. Agar. alco. Alet. alf. all-s. alum-p. alum-sil. Alum. alumn. am-c. am-caust. am-m. Ambr. ambro. anac. androc. ang. ant-c. ant-t. anthraci. Apis apoc. aq-mar. Arg-met. Arg-n. arn. ARS-I. ars-met. ars-s-f. ARS. arum-i. asc-t. astra-e. astra-m. aur-ar. aur-m. Aur. bac. bapt. bar-act. BAR-C. bar-i. Bar-m. bar-s. Bell. ben-n. benz-ac. beryl. bism. borx. both. brach. brass-n-o. Brom. Bry. Bufo buni-o. Cact. calc-ar. calc-f. calc-hp. CALC-I. calc-m. calc-ox. Calc-p. Calc-sil. CALC. Camph. cann-s. Canth. Caps. Carb-an. Carb-v. carbn-o. Carbn-s. carc. carl. carneg-g. Caust.

cench. cere-b. Cetr. Cham. Chel. CHIN. chinin-ar. chinin-s. Chion. chlol. Chlor. cic. cimic. cina Cist. Clem. cob-n. coca Cocc. coff. Colch. Coloc. con. cor-r. cordyc. cory. Crot-c. crot-t. cub. cund. Cupr. dig. digin. diphtox. dros. dulc. echi. echit. euphr. eupi. Ferr-ar. Ferr-i. Ferr-m. ferr-p. FERR. Fl-ac. fuc. gaert. Gamb. gels. germ-met. Glycyr-g. gran. GRAPH. Guaj. haliae-lc. hed. HELL. helo-s. helo. Helon. Hep. Hippoz. hura Hydr. hydrog. Ign. IOD. Ip. jal. jug-c. kali-ar. kali-bi. Kali-br. Kali-c. Kali-i. Kali-p. kali-s. Kali-sil. kali-t. Kreos. kres. Lac-ac. lac-c. Lac-d. Lach. lat-k. lat-m. Laur. lec. led. lil-t. Lith-c. luf-op. LYC. Lycps-v. lyss. mag-c. mag-m. mag-p. mang-act. mang. med. Merc-c. merc-k-i. Merc. mez. moly-met. morph. Mucor Mur-ac. myos-a. Myos-s. naja Nat-ar. Nat-c. NAT-HCHLS. NAT-M. Nat-n. Nat-p. Nat-s. nat-sil. Nicc. NIT-AC. nit-s-d. nuph. nux-m. NUX-V. Ol-j. Op. ox-ac. ozone parathyr. pers. Petr. Ph-ac. phel. PHOS. Phyt. pic-ac. pilo. pin-s. pip-m. Plan. plb-xyz. PLB. Podo. Psor. Puls. pyrog. raph. Rheum rhus-g. Rhus-t. rhus-v. Rumx. ruta sacch. samb. Sanic. saroth. Sars. Sec. SEL. Senec. sep. SIL. spig. spong. Stann-i. STANN. staph. still. Stram. Strept-ent. Stront-c. Sul-ac. sul-h. sul-i. sulfa. SULPH. sumb. symph. Syph. syzyg. tab. Tarent. Ter. Teucr. thal-xyz. thal. ther. thuj-l. Thuj. thyr. tritic-vg. tub-a. tub-m. tub-r. TUB. uran-met. uran-n. v-a-b. vanad. vanil. Verat-v. Verat. vesp. vip. voes. x-ray zinc-m. zinc-val. Zinc. Zinc.

GENERALS - INFLAMMATION - Bones; of

Acon. Ang. ars-i. ars. Asaf. aur-ar. aur-i. Aur-m. aur-s. aur. Bell. bry. calc-f. calc-sil. Calc. chin. clem. coloc. con. conch. cupr. dig. dys. euph. FL-AC. guaj. hecla hep. iod. Kali-i. kreos. Lac-ac. lach. Lyc. mag-m. mang-act. Mang. merc-c. merc-k-i. merc-sul. MERC. MEZ. nat-c. nat-sil. Nit-ac. PH-AC. Phos. Phyt. plb. Psor. PULS. rhus-t. sep. SIL. spig. STAPH. staphycoc. still. stront-c. Sulph. Symph. thuj. tub-m. tub. verat.

GENERALS - SWELLING - Glands; of

abrot. acon-l. acon. Aesc. aeth. agn. Ail. Aln. alum-sil. alum. Alumn. am-c. Am-m. ambr. ancis-p. ant-c. ant-t. Anthraci. Apis aq-mar. arg-met. arn. ARS-I. ars-s-f. Ars. Arum-t. asaf. astac. aur-ar. aur-i. Aur-m. aur-s. aur. Bad. Bapt. BAR-C. BAR-I. BAR-M. bar-

s. BELL. Berb. bit-ar. borx. both-ax. both. bov. BROM. Bry. Bufo calad. calc-ar. Calc-f. calc-hp. CALC-I. calc-m. calc-p. CALC-S. Calc-sil. Calc. Calen. camph. cann-s. Canth. caps. CARB-AN. CARB-V. Carbn-s. carc. caust. cench. Cham. chim. chin. cic. cinnb. CIST. CLEM. cloth. coc-c. cocc. coloc. CON. cor-r. cory. croc. crot-c. crot-h. cupr. cycl. dig. dros. DULC. Eucal. euph. euphr. eupi. ferr-ar. ferr-i. FERR. fl-ac. fuc. GRAPH. hall ham. Hecla hed. hell. HEP. hippoz. hydrc. hyos. ign. IOD. Iris jug-r. Kali-ar. Kali-bi. kali-br. Kali-c. Kali-chl. Kali-i. kali-m. kreos. lac-c. lach. Lap-a. lat-m. led. Lith-c. LYC. mag-c. mag-m. mang. med. MERC-C. merc-d. Merc-i-f. Merc-i-r. merc-k-i. MERC. mez. mur-ac. Nat-c. nat-m. Nat-p. nat-s. NIT-AC. Nux-v. ol-j. ozone petr. Ph-ac. PHOS. Phyt. plb. psor. Puls. pyrog. ran-b. ran-s. raph. rhod. RHUS-T. Rumx. ruta sabad. sabin. samb. sars. scir. scol. scroph-n. sec. Sep. sil-mar. SIL. sol-a. sol-o. spig. SPONG. squil. Stann. staph. stict. stram. streptoc. stront-c. Sul-ac. Sul-i. SULPH. symph. Syph. tab. tarent. ter. teucr. ther. thiosin. THUJ. toxo-g. tub-a. tub-m. Tub. uran-n. urea v-a-b. Verat. viol-o. viol-t. vip. Zinc.

GENERALS - SWELLING - Glands; of - painless

ars. asaf. CALC. cocc. Con. cycl. dulc. Ign. lach. merc. Nit-ac. Ph-ac. plb. Sep. sil. staph. sulph. thuj. Tub.

GENERALS - WEAKNESS

abies-c. abies-n. abrom-a. abrot. absin. Acet-ac. Acetan. achy. acon-c. acon-f. Acon. adam. adlu. Adon. adox. adren. aesc-g. aesc. Aeth. aether agar-cpn. agar-em. agar-pa. Agar-ph. agar-pr. agar-st. agar. agath-a. agav-t. Agn. aids. ail. alco. Alet. alf. all-c. all-s. allox. aln. Aloe alst-s. alst. alum-p. alum-sil. Alum. alumn. am-br. AM-C. am-caust. am-m. Ambr. Aml-ns. ammc. amor-r. amph. amyg. ANAC. Anag. anan. ancis-p. androc. Ang. anil. Ant-ar. Ant-c. ant-m. ant-o. ANT-T. anth. anthraci. anthraco. anthraq. Antip. aphis APIS apoc-a. apoc. apom. aq-mar. aq-pet. ara-maca. aral. aran-sc. Aran. arg-cy. ARG-MET. Arg-n. arist-cl. ARN. ars-h. ars-i. Ars-met. ars-s-f. ars-s-r. ARS. arum-d. arum-i. arum-m. arum-t. asaf. asar. asc-t. asim. aspar. astac. aster. atha. atra-r. atro. aur-ar. aur-fu. aur-m-n. Aur-m. aur-s. Aur. Aven. bac. bacls-7. Bals-p. BAPT. bar-act.

BAR-C. bar-i. Bar-m. bar-ox-suc. bart. bell-p. bell. ben-n. ben. Benz-ac. berb. berbin. beryl. bism-o. Bism. Bit-ar. Bol-la. bol-s. borx. Both. bov. brach. brass-n-o. BROM. bruc. brucel. brucin. Bry. bufo bung-fa. buni-o. buth-a. Cact. cadm-met. cadm-s. cain. caj. calad. calc-ar. calc-caust. calc-hp. CALC-I. calc-m. calc-p. calc-s. calc-sil. CALC. Camph. cann-i. cann-s. Canth. canthin. caps. car. CARB-AC. Carb-an. carb-v. carbn-chl. carbn-h. carbn-o. Carbn-s. carc. card-m. Carl. cartl-s. casc. cass. cassia-s. castm. castn-v. Caul. Caust. cedr. cench. cent. cere-b. cerv. Cham. chap. CHEL. chelo. Chim. CHIN. chinin-ar. Chinin-fcit. CHININ-S. chion. chir-fl. chlam-tr. chlf. chlol. chloram. chlorpr. choc. chord-umb. chr-ac. Cic. cich. cimic. cimx. Cina cinnb. cinnm. cist. cit-l. cit-v. Clem. Cloth. cob-n. cob. coc-c. COCA Cocc. coch. cod. Coff. COLCH. colchin. Coli. coll. coloc. colocin. colum-p. com. CON. conin-br. conin. conv. cop. cor-r. cordyc. corian-s. corn-a. corn. cortico. cortiso. cot. crat. croc. Crot-c. Crot-h. Crot-t. cub. culx. cupr-act. Cupr-ar. cupr-s. Cupr. cur. Cycl. cyn-d. cypr. cypra-eg. cystein-l. cyt-l. Daph. dendr-pol. der. dicha. DIG. Digin. digox. dios. dip. diph. diphtox. dirc. dor. Dros. dubo-m. Dulc. Echi. elaps elat. ephe-si. equis-h. erig. ery-a. ery-m. eryt-j. esch. eucal. eug. eup-per. eup-pur. euph-a. euph-c. euph-hy. euph-ip. euph. euphr. eupi. fab. fago. fagu. ferr-ar. FERR-I. FERR-M. ferr-ma. Ferr-p. ferr-pic. ferr. fic-m. fic-r. fil. Fl-ac. flor-p. Form. frag. franz. Fum. fuma-ac. gad. gal-ac. galeg. galin. galla-q-r. Gamb. gard-j. gast. GELS. gent-l. gent-q. germ-met. get. gink-b. gins. glon. glyc. Glycyr-g. goss. gran. Granit-m. GRAPH. grat. guaj. guan. guar. guare. haem. haliae-lc. hall Ham. hed. hedeo. hell-o. Hell. helo-s. helo. helodr-cal. helon. HEP. hera. hip-ac. Hipp. hippoc-k. hir. hist. home. hura Hydr-ac. Hydr. Hydrc. Hydrog. hydroph. HYOS. hyosin. Hyper. iber. Ign. ind. indg. IOD. Ip. Irid-met. iris jab. jal. jasm. jatr-c. jug-c. jug-r. juni-v. KALI-AR. Kali-bi. Kali-br. KALI-C. kali-chl. kali-cy. KALI-FCY. Kali-i. kali-m. kali-n. kali-ox. KALI-P. kali-perm. kali-s. kali-sil. kali-sula. kali-t. KALM. ketogl-ac. kino kiss. kola kou. kreos. kres. lac-ac. Lac-c. Lac-d. lac-del. lac-h. Lac-leo. LACH. lachn. lact. lam. lap-la. lapa. lat-h. lat-k. lat-m. LAUR. LEC. led. lepi. lept. lev. lil-s. lil-t. lim. limest-b. lina. linu-c. lipp.

lith-c. lith-chl. lob-c. lob-p. lob-s. lob. lobin. Lol. loxo-lae. loxo-recl. luf-op. LUNA Lyc. lycps-v. lyss. m-ambo. m-arct. m-aust. macro. mag-c. mag-f. mag-m. Mag-p. mag-s. magn-gr. maland. malar. manc. mand. mang-o. mang-p. mang. MED. mela. melal-alt. meli. menis. meny. meph. merc-br. MERC-C. MERC-CY. merc-d. merc-i-f. merc-i-r. merc-k-i. merc-meth. merc-ns. merc-sul. MERC. merl. methys. mez. mill. mim-p. mit. moly-met. Mom-b. Moni. morph. mosch. MUR-AC. murx. musca-d. mygal. Myric. nabal. naja napht. narcin. narz. nat-ar. Nat-c. Nat-chl. nat-f. NAT-HCHLS. nat-lac. NAT-M. nat-n. NAT-P. NAT-S. Nat-sal. nat-sil. nat-sula. nauf-helv-li. nep. nept-m. nicc-met. nicc-s. nicc. nicot. nid. nig-s. NIT-AC. nit-m-ac. nit-s-d. nitro-o. nuph. Nux-m. Nux-v. oci-sa. oena. okou. ol-an. Ol-j. Olib-sac. OLND. onos. op. opun-v. orch. orig. orni. orot-ac. osm. ost. osteo-a. Ox-ac. oxal-a. oxyg. ozone paeon. pall. palo. par. parathyr. parth. paull. ped. penic. perh. pert. petr-ra. Petr. PH-AC. phal. phel. PHOS. Phys. physal-al. Phyt. PIC-AC. pilo. pimp. pin-con. pip-m. pitu-gl. pitu-p. pitu. pix plac-s. plan. Plat. plb-chr. PLB. plect. plumbg. plut-n. pneu. podo. polyg-h. polyp-p. polys. Positr. Prim-o. Propr. prun-p. psil. PSOR. ptel. puls-n. Puls. pulx. Pycnop-sa. pyrid. pyrog. pyrus querc-r. rad-br. ran-a. RAN-B. ran-s. Raph. rat. rham-f. rheum rhod. rhodi. rhus-g. RHUS-T. Rhus-v. ribo. ric. Rob. Rosm. rumx-act. Rumx. ruta Sabad. sabal sabin. sacch-a. sacch. salin. samb-c. samb. Sang. sanguis-s. Sanic. santin. sapin. Sarcol-ac. saroth. sarr. Sars. scarl. Scor. scroph-n. scut. SEC. SEL. senec. Seneg. senn. SEP. sieg. SIL. silphu. sin-n. sinus. sium sol-mm. sol-ni. sol-t-ae. sol-t. solid. solin. sphing. spig. spira. spirae. Spong. SQUIL. STANN. STAPH. staphycoc. Stict. still. Stram. stront-c. stroph-h. stry-p. stry. suis-pan. SUL-AC. sul-h. sul-i. sulfa. Sulfon. sulfonam. SULPH. sumb. suprar. symph. syph. syzyg. TAB. tanac. tang. tann-ac. tarax. tarent-c. TARENT. tart-ac. tax. Tell. TER. tere-ch. teucr. thal. thea Ther. thiop.. Thuj. thymol. thyr. til. toxo-g. trach. tril-p. tritic-vg. trom. tub-d. tub-r. tub-sp. TUB. tus-p. uncar-tom. upa. uran-met. uran-n. urea ust. uva v-a-b. vac. valer. vanil. ven-m. verat-v. VERAT. verb. vesp. vib. vinc. viol-o. viol-t. vip-a-c. vip-a. vip-d. vip. visc. voes. wies. wildb. wye. x-ray xan. Zinc-ar. zinc-m. zinc-p.

Zinc-pic. zinc-s. Zinc. zing. ziz.

CHAPTER FIFTEEN

BIBLIOGRAPHY

- Another important consideration in this group is sarcoid myelopathy (Chap. 322), in which an...- Harrison's Online > Chapter 372. Diseases of the Spinal Cord > Acute and Subacute Spinal Cord Diseases > Noncompressive Myelopathies > Inflammatory and Immune Myelopathies (Myelitis) > Systemic Inflammatory Disorders
- Chapter 153. Sarcoidosis- Dermatology
- Chapter 322. Sarcoidosis- Harrison's Online
- Chapter 53. Sarcoidosis- CURRENT Rheumatology Diagnosis & Treatment
- Figure e10-78. A. Sarcoid. Infiltrated papules and plaques of variable...- Harrison's Online > Chapter e10. Atlas of Skin Manifestations of Internal Disease > Skin Manifestations of Internal Disease
- Figure e24-18. Sarcoid—CXR of stage I (hilar lymphadenopathy without parenchymal...- Harrison's Online > Chapter e24. Atlas of Chest Imaging > Interstitial Processes
- Figure e24-19. Sarcoid—CT scan of stage I demonstrating bulky hilar and mediastinal...- Harrison's Online > Chapter e24. Atlas of Chest Imaging > Interstitial Processes
- Figure e24-21. Sarcoid—CT scan of stage II (calcified lymphadenopathy, parenchymal...- Harrison's Online > Chapter e24. Atlas of Chest Imaging > Interstitial Processes

- Figure e24-22. Sarcoid—CT scan of stage II (nodular opacities tracking along...- Harrison's Online > Chapter e24. Atlas of Chest Imaging > Interstitial Processes
- Figure e24-23. Sarcoid—stage III with nodular parenchymal infiltrates (yellow arrows...- Harrison's Online > Chapter e24. Atlas of Chest Imaging > Interstitial Processes
- Figure e24-24. Sarcoid—stage IV (fibrotic lung disease).- Harrison's Online > Chapter e24. Atlas of Chest Imaging > Interstitial Processes
- Figure e9-27. Sarcoidosis. There is chronic interstitial nephritis with numerous, confluent,...- Harrison's Online > Chapter e9. Atlas of Urinary Sediments and Renal Biopsies > Atlas of Renal Biopsies and Urinary Sediments
- Granulomatous Processes- CURRENT Rheumatology Diagnosis & Treatment > Chapter 51. Evaluation of Rheumatic Complaints in Patients with HIV > Sicca Syndrome > Differential Diagnosis
- Key Syndrome Sarcoidosis- DeGowin's Diagnostic Examination > Chapter 8. The Chest: Chest Wall, Pulmonary, and Cardiovascular Systems; The Breasts > Chest Wall, Pulmonary, and Cardiovascular Systems > Chest, Cardiovascular and Respiratory Syndromes > Respiratory Syndromes
- Nodular Dermatitis: Sarcoidosis- Pathophysiology of Disease > Chapter 8. Diseases of the Skin > Pathophysiology of Selected Skin Diseases
- Sarcoidosis & Other Granulomatous Disorders- Greenspan's Basic & Clinical Endocrinology > Chapter 9. Metabolic Bone Disease > Hypercalcemia > Disorders Causing Hypercalcemia
- Sarcoidosis (Boeck Sarcoid, Benign Lymphogranulomatosis)- CURRENT Diagnosis & Treatment: Surgery, 13e > Chapter 18. Thoracic Wall, Pleura, Mediastinum, & Lung > Diseases of the Lungs
- Sarcoidosis- Adams and Victor's Neurology > Chapter 46. Diseases of the Peripheral Nerves > Asymmetrical and Multifocal Polyneuropathies (Mononeuropathy, or Mononeuritis Multiplex) > Vasculitic Neuropathies

- Sarcoidosis and Other Granulomatous Diseases- Harrison's Online > Chapter 347. Diseases of the Parathyroid Gland and Other Hyper- and Hypocalcemic Disorders > Hypercalcemia > Vitamin D–Related Hypercalcemia
- Sarcoidosis and Other Granulomatous Disorders- CURRENT Medical Dx & Tx > Chapter 26. Endocrine Disorders > The Parathyroids > Hyperparathyroidism > Differential Diagnosis
- Sarcoidosis- Clinical Neurology > Chapter 6. Disorders of Somatic Sensation > Polyneuropathies > Infective & Granulomatous Neuropathies
- Sarcoidosis- CURRENT Diagnosis & Treatment in Cardiology > Chapter 16. Myocarditis > Specific Forms of Myocarditis
- Sarcoidosis- CURRENT Diagnosis & Treatment in Otolaryngology > Chapter 17. Benign Diseases of the Salivary Glands > Nonneoplastic Diseases > Chronic Granulomatous Sialadenitis > Differential Diagnosis
- Sarcoidosis- CURRENT Diagnosis & Treatment in Otolaryngology > Chapter 29. Benign Laryngeal Lesions > Rare Laryngeal Lesions
- Sarcoidosis- CURRENT Diagnosis & Treatment in Otolaryngology > Chapter 12. Nasal Manifestations of Systemic Disease > Granulomatous & Autoimmune Diseases
- Sarcoidosis- CURRENT Diagnosis & Treatment in Otolaryngology > Chapter 26. Neck Masses > Inflammatory Neck Masses > Infectious Inflammatory Disorders > Granulomatous Diseases
- Sarcoidosis- CURRENT Medical Dx & Tx > Chapter 24. Nervous System Disorders > Peripheral Neuropathies > Polyneuropathies & Mononeuritis Multiplex > Neuropathies Associated With Infectious & Inflammatory Diseases
- Sarcoidosis- CURRENT Medical Dx & Tx > Chapter 9. Pulmonary Disorders > Interstitial Lung Disease (Diffuse Parenchymal Lung Disease)
- Sarcoidosis- Dermatology > Chapter 151. The Skin and Disorders of the Alimentary Tract, the Hepatobiliary System,

Kidney, and Cardiopulmonary System > Specific Organ and System Changes > Respiratory System

- Sarcoidosis- Dermatology > Chapter 227. Aminoquinolines > Indications
- Sarcoidosis- Dermatology > Chapter 73. Hypomelanoses and Hypermelanoses > Hypomelanosis > Acquired Localized Hypomelanosis
- Sarcoidosis- Goodman & Gilman's Pharmacology > Chapter 59. Adrenocorticotropic Hormone; Adrenocortical Steroids and Their Synthetic Analogs; Inhibitors of the Synthesis and Actions of Adrenocortical Hormones > Adrenocortical Steroids > Therapeutic Uses > Therapeutic Uses in Nonendocrine Diseases > Miscellaneous Diseases and Conditions
- Sarcoidosis- Greenspan's Basic & Clinical Endocrinology > Chapter 5. Hypothalamus & Pituitary Gland > Pituitary & Hypothalamic Disorders > Hypopituitarism > Etiology > Infiltrative
- Sarcoidosis- Harrison's Online > Chapter 244. Pulmonary Hypertension > Other Disorders Directly Affecting Pulmonary Vasculature
- Sarcoidosis- Hurst's The Heart > Chapter 21. Magnetic Resonance Imaging of the Heart > Clinical Applications > Heart Failure and Cardiomyopathies
- Sarcoidosis is a systemic granulomatous disorder that characteristically affects the mediastinal ...- CURRENT Diagnosis & Treatment in Pulmonary Medicine > Chapter 24. Diseases of the Mediastinum > Pathogenesis > Lymphatic
- Sarcoidosis- Schwartz's Principles of Surgery > Chapter 34. Spleen > Indications for Splenectomy > Storage Diseases and Infiltrative Disorders
- Sarcoidosis- Vaughan & Asbury's General Opthalmology > Chapter 15. Ocular Disorders Associated with Systemic Diseases > Granulomatous Diseases
- Sarcoidosis- Williams Obstetrics, 23e > Chapter 46. Pulmonary Disorders

- Sarcoidosis-Vaughan & Asbury's General Opthalmology > Chapter 7. Uveal Tract & Sclera > Uveal Tract > Uveitis > Diffuse Uveitis (Table 7–6)
- Sinonasal Inflammatory Disease (Wegener Granulomatosis & Sarcoidosis)- CURRENT Medical Dx & Tx > Chapter 8. Ear, Nose, & Throat Disorders > Tumors & Granulomatous Disease
- Table 234-1 Common Systemic Disorders and Their Associated Cardiac- Manifestations- Harrison's Online > Chapter 234. Cardiac Manifestations of Systemic Disease > Cardiac Manifestations of Systemic Disease: Introduction
- The cutaneous lesions in sarcoidosis (Chap. 322) are classically red to red-brown in color,...- Harrison's Online > Chapter 54. Skin Manifestations of Internal Disease > Papulonodular Skin Lesions > Red-Brown Lesions
- The differential diagnosis of sarcoidosis includes foreign-body granulomas produced by chemicals...- Harrison's Online > Chapter 54. Skin Manifestations of Internal Disease > Papulonodular Skin Lesions > Red-Brown Lesions
- Ventricular Tachycardia in Cardiac Sarcoidosis- Hurst's The Heart > Chapter 39. Ventricular Arrhythmias > Ventricular Tachycardia in Patients with Nonischemic Cardiomyopathy
- While pulmonary involvement in sarcoidosis is extremely common, laryngeal disease is relatively rar...- Principles of Critical Care > Chapter 34. Upper Airway Obstruction > Causes of Upper Airway Obstruction > Laryngeal Causes > Miscellaneous Causes
- Chapter 12. Sarcoidosis- CURRENT Diagnosis & Treatment in Pulmonary Medicine
- Encyclopedia Homoeopathica
- Figure e24-20. Sarcoid—CXR of stage II (lymphadenopathy with parenchymal changes). Note...- Harrison's Online > Chapter e24. Atlas of Chest Imaging > Interstitial Processes
- Opus
- Radar 10

- Sarcoidosis- Adams and Victor's Neurology > Chapter 32. Infections of the Nervous System (Bacterial, Fungal, Spirochetal, Parasitic) and Sarcoidosis > Subacute and Chronic Forms of Meningitis
- Sarcoidosis- CURRENT Diagnosis & Treatment: Surgery, 13e > Chapter 27. Spleen > Operative Indications for Splenectomy > Metabolic Disorders
- Sarcoidosis- Fitzpatrick's Color Atlas and Synopsis of Clinical Dermatology > Section 14. The Skin in Immune, Autoimmune, and Rheumatic Disorders
- Sarcoidosis- Hurst's The Heart > Chapter 31. Restrictive, Obliterative, and Infiltrative Cardiomyopathies > Specific Restrictive Cardiomyopathic Diseases > Myocardial Diseases > Infiltrative Cardiomyopathies
- A case based guide to clinical endocrinology – p- 26, 175, 259, 404
- Allen, H. C. - Keynotes and Characteristics with Comparisons of Some of The Leading Remedies
- Allen, H. C. – Materia Medical of some important Nosodes
- Allen, J. H., The Chronic Miasms, B. Jain Publishers (P.) Ltd., New
- Anatomy – side by side- P- 125
- Antibiotics- 2005- P- 8
- Atlas of clinical oncology of endocrine tumors- P- 148
- Banerjea, Subrata Kumar- Miasmatic Diagnosis, Revised Edition, 2003
- Banerjee, D. D. (New Edition)- A Text Book of Homoeopathic Pharmacy- p. 47-50
- Banerjee, S. K. - Miasmatic Diagnosis Practical Tips with Clinical Comparisons, B. Jain Publishers (P.) Ltd., New Delhi, Revised Edition 2003.
- Benerjee, D. - The Glimpses of History of Medicine- p. 1, 4, 10-12, 14-15, 18, 21, 27, 33, 45, 49, 52
- Bernoville, Fortier - What We Must Not Do In Homoeopathy

- Blackwood, A.– A manual of Materia Medica, Therapeutics and Pharmacology
- Boericke, William - Pocket Manual of Homoeopathic Materia Medica & Repertory, B. Jain Publishers (P.) Ltd., New Delhi, Reprint Edition 1999
- Boerricke, Oscar - Repertory
- Boger C. M., Boenninghaussen - Boger C. Boenninghaussen's Repertory
- Boger, C. M. – A Synoptic Key of the Materia Medica
- Burt, W. H. – Physiological Materia Medica
- Chaddha, P. V. - Hand book of Experimental Physiology & Biochemistry
- Chaterjee, Chandi Charan - Human Physiology, 11th Edition
- Chaudhury, K. - Practice of Medicine
- Choudhary, Harimohan - Indications of Miasm, B. Jain Publishers (P) Ltd., New Delhi, Reprint Edition 1994
- Choudhury, N. M. - A Study on Materia Medica
- Clarke, G. H., The ABC Manual of Materia Medica & Therapeutics
- Clarke, J. H. - Clinical Repertory
- Clarke, J. H. - Homoeopathy Explained, B. Jain Publishers (P.) Ltd. New Delhi, Reprint Edition 1995
- Clarke, John Henry - A Dictionary of Practical Materia Medica (Vol. 1 to 3)- B. Jain Publishers (P.) Ltd., New Delhi, Reprint Edition 2000
- Clarke, John Henry - Non Surgical Treatment of Diseases of the Glands & Bones with a Chapter on Scrofula
- Clause, Stuart - The Genius Of Homoeopathy
- Clinical pathology course hand book – KEM Turner- P- 15, 26
- Clinical physiology – Ashish Banerjee- p - 185
- Common Laboratory Tests P – 29, 63, 67, 203
- Cowperthwaite, A. C. - A Textbook of Materia Medica & Therapeutics, B. Jain Publishers (P) Ltd., New
- Das, K. – Handbook of Surgery, 5th Edition
- Das, K.- Clinical Methods in surgery

- Davidson's Principles and Practice of Medicine, Delhi, Reprint Edition, 1988
- Dewey, W. A. - Essentials of Homoeopathic Therapeutics, B. Jain Publishers (P) Ltd., New Delhi, Reprint Edition 1981
- Dewhurst Text book of obs and gyne- 7th ed. P- 405, 409
- Drug Today 2007
- Encyclopedia of Endocrine diseases and disorders- p- 144
- Encyclopedia of endocrinology- P- 82, 646, 1105, 1215, 1238, 1247, 2173, 2374
- Farrington, E. A. - Clinical Materia Medica
- Farrington, E. A. - Comparative Materia Medica
- Farrington, E. A. - Therapeutic Pointers
- Guide to common laboratory tests- p- 3, 7, 21, 23, 25, 34
- Gunavante, S. M. - The Genius of Homoeopahic Remedies
- Gupta, A. C. - Organon of Medicine, At A Glance, Part I & II
- Gupta, S. P., Dr. A. K. Gupta- Medical Emergencies In General Practice
- Hahnemann, Samuel - Organon of Medicine, B. Jain Publishers (P) Ltd., New Delhi 6th Edition Reprint Edition 1996
- Hahnemann, Samuel, The Chronic Diseases, Their Peculiar Nature & Their homoeopathic Cure, B. Jain Publishers (P) Ltd., New Delhi 5th Edition
- Hand book of diagnostic endocrinology- P- 50, 67, 253, 255, 314
- Harrison' Principles of Internal Medicine, 11th Edition
- Harrison' Principles of Internal Medicine, 11th Edition, Vol. II
- Herbert A. Roberts- The Principles & Art of Cure by Homoeopathy
- Hering, C., The Guiding Symptoms of our Materia Medica Vol. 1 to 10, Reprint Edition 1993
- Hoyne, T. S. - Clinical Therapeutics, B. Jain Publishers (P) Ltd., New Delhi, Vol. I & II, Reprint Edition 1993
- Hughes, R. and Dake J. P. - A Cyclopedia of Drug Pathogenesy
- Introduction to analytical Chemistry- I Ebdon-P 4
- Julian, O. A. – Materia Medica of New Homoeopathic Remedies
- Kanodia, K. D. - Danger Zones In Homoeopathy

- Kent, J. T. - Lectures on Materia Medica, B. Jain Publishers (P) Ltd., New Delhi
- Kent, J. T. - Repertory Of Homoeopathic Materia Medica
- Kent, J. T. - Repertory of the Homoeopathic Materia Medica, B. Jain Publishers (P) Ltd., New Delhi, Reprint Edition 2001
- Kent, James Tyler - Lectures on Homoeopathic Materia Medica
- Laboratory notes guide to laboratory and diagnostic tests- 2005- Hopkins- P – 44
- Landes Bioscience breast diseases- P- 84
- Lesser, O. – Text Book of Homoeopathic Materia Medica
- Lilienthal, S., - Homoeopathic Therapeutics
- Lippe, Adolph Von. – Key Notes and Redline Symptoms of the Materia Medica
- Lippe, Adolph Von. – Text Book of Materia Medica
- Mohan, Harsh-Text Book of Pathology, Jaypee Bro. Medical Publishers (P) Ltd. 5th edition
- Murphy, Robin - Lotus Materia Medica, B. Jain Publishers (P) Ltd., New Delhi, 2nd Revised Edition
- Nash, E. B. - How to Take the Case & To Find the Similimum- p. 2- 14
- Nash, E. B. - Leaders in Homoeopathic Therapeutics
- Oxford hand book of chemical and laboratory investigations- P- 43,48, 61, 89, 94, 97, 128, 311, 528
- Patel, R. P., Chronic Miasms in Homoeopathy & Their Cure
- Pathology side by side – p- 177, 178, 181, 191, 301
- Phatak, S. R. - Concise Repertory
- Phatak, S. R. – Materia Medica of Homoeopathic Medicines
- Pollock, Anshutz Edward - New Old & Forgotten Remedies, B. Jain Publishers (P) Ltd., New Delhi, Reprint Edition 1987
- Robert, Herbert A. - Sensations As If....
- Robins Pathological basis of diseases- 7th Ed. P- 661, 662, 667, 795, 803, 834, 1501
- Schroyens, Frederick - Synthesis 9.2.1b
- Schwabe, Willmar - Practical Homoeopathy in Every Day Medical Practice

- Sircar, S. D. - Organon Expositor
- Speight, Phyllis- A comparison of the Chronic Miasms B. Jain Publishers (P) Ltd., New Delhi, Reprint Edition - 1998
- Taber's Cyclopedic Medical Dictionary
- Taylor M. L. - Homoeopathy, Introductory Lectures
- The Concise Oxford Dictionary
- Tierney, Lawrence M., Stephen J. McPhee- Current Medical Diagnosis & Treatment
- Verma, P. N. - Materia Medica in Tabular Form
- Vithoulkas, G., - Materia Medica Viva
- Vithoulkas, George - Science of Homoeopathy
- Vol. I, II, III, IV, V, VI- Homoeopathic Pharmacopoeia of India
- Vols. I, II & III- Synthetic Repertory
- Weatherrall, Ledingham, Warrel, Oxford Textbook of Medicine, Oxford Medical Publications, 3rd edition
- www.cchindia.org
- www.emedicine.com
- www.healthonline.com
- www.healthorg.com
- www.hmc.org
- www.homegci.net
- www.hommiasm.com
- www.homoeopathy.com
- www.hpathy.com
- www.library.med.utah.edu/kw/human_reprod/lectures/ clinical_genetics/index.html
- www.medsafe.govt.nz
- www.pmjonline.com
- www.qis.net
- www.thenewmedicine.org
- www.touregypt.net
- www.whonamedit.com
- Yingling, W. A. – Accouncheurs Emergency Manual

www.ingramcontent.com/pod-product-compliance
Lightning Source LLC
Chambersburg PA
CBHW041335120726
48005CB00014B/2260